Rosa Luxemburg

Titles in the series Critical Lives present the work of leading cultural figures of the modern period. Each book explores the life of the artist, writer, philosopher or architect in question and relates it to their major works.

In the same series

Rosa Luxemburg

Dana Mills

REAKTION BOOKS

For my mother, Gabriela Mills, my aunt, Tirza Posner, and in memory of my grandmother, Annemarie (Miriam) Posner

Published by
REAKTION BOOKS LTD
Unit 32, Waterside
44–48 Wharf Road
London N1 7UX, UK

www.reaktionbooks.co.uk

First published 2020
Copyright © Dana Mills 2020

Printed and bound in Great Britain by Bell & Bain Ltd, Glasgow

A catalogue record for this book is available from the British Library

ISBN 978 1 78914 327 0

Contents

Rosa Luxemburg, 1912. 'History will do its work. See that you too do your work,' she wrote in 1913.

Introduction

A century after Rosa Luxemburg's death, her revolutionary heart beats loudly still. Rosa Luxemburg was an internationalist and foremost thinker of democracy within the Marxist tradition, an anti-imperialist, anti-militarist revolutionary in theory and action. Luxemburg lived her life in anticipation of a better tomorrow. A pioneer in understanding the interconnectivity of injustices and working towards a just world, she was a woman of fiercely independent thought and action. Rosa Luxemburg had a uniquely brilliant mind and an inimitable personality. Her time was truly revolutionary, and she embodied the revolutionary energy of the time.

The themes for which she agitated all her life still occupy our front pages, a century after she dramatically left the earth. A central reason why Rosa Luxemburg speaks to us so profoundly these days is that she never fitted the boxes of her own definition of identity, and refused to see others as fitting into specific boxes either. At the same time, it is her raw humanity, her flaws and contradictions, that makes her work compelling for us today. She was entrenched in studying what it means to be human, and how we, as human beings, can work to make a better world.

This book re-examines the legacy and teachings of Rosa Luxemburg as it examines the truly singular way in which her life unfolded. Beyond exploring her position as a significant Marxist theorist – 'the best brain after Marx', according to her comrade

Franz Mehring[1] – this biography considers the intertwined elements of her legacy, life and work that are significant for our own work towards a just world today.

A revolutionary in more ways than one, Luxemburg was a freethinker who subverted the conversations in which she took part. Thus this study of her work tries to engage both points of view. How did her ideas intervene in discourses of her time, and how do they intervene in our own time, a century after her untimely death? It is written from interweaving temporalities; it asks to be attentive to Rosa's own time, illuminating how extraordinary she was in her day, as well as re-examining her work from our own position in the early twenty-first century, showing the colossal legacy she has left for us.

Rosa was a woman, a Pole and a Jewess, agitating in a world in which she herself was treated with gross inequality and targeted with manifold forms of racism and oppression. And yet she worked ceaselessly towards a just and equal world for all. Her emphasis on humanity and insistence on revolution gave coherence to a fraught life and a colossal economic and political legacy. This book brings to centre stage the question of the place of empathy in politics today as well as in Luxemburg's time. Her main commandment to herself was 'to be good'.[2] Luxemburg's work as an anti-war campaigner, anti-imperialist and anti-racist stems from her ability to see the world from others' point of view. Her view of the world set an agenda that included a radically new understanding of the relationship between social democracy, human rights and environmental justice. In many cases the people through whom she viewed the world were ones she would never meet; she could only use her emotional and intellectual imaginaries to think about their place in her most proximate world. She was, herself, an outsider – what Hannah Arendt would term elsewhere 'a pariah'[3] – and yet her politics were never limited to those of similar identity. This unique position encourages us especially in our contemporary moment, a century after her murder, to consider our own imaginaries and their limitations.

Rosa was a generous friend and a passionate lover. She was committed to the cause for which she spent her life agitating and yet her life outside of that activism was equally full and contradictory. Rosa had a multifaceted personality, the contradictions in her personal life leaving us with many unresolved questions. This book, as a study of both Rosa's life and work, allows for those intermeshing lines to unravel. A true advocate for humanity, she never ceased to question in herself what it means to be human. Rosa was witty, sharp and charismatic. An extraordinary emotional depth that plunged her into dark moods also allowed her to capture the world – with its beauty and ugliness – in a unique way. Rosa's resilience and determination shone through her many ups and downs. It is Rosa's faith in humanity that motivates this study.

Rosa Luxemburg is still, in many ways, in our political landscapes. She always thought ahead of where she was at present; aptly, Rosa loved walking – she bonded with people while walking and would joke about her small stature, which demanded larger strides: 'I can see the way you're smiling wickedly at how small I am, I see it, (I.E. too small for such a walk).'[4] Rosa kept a strict walking discipline throughout her life, despite the fact that it was only when she walked that it became apparent she was disabled. This is telling of the strength of her will, her sense of humour, and her commitment to the inseparability of the human and natural world, but, more than anything, to setting her eyes on the future horizon to which she was marching.

Rosa's understanding of freedom developed later in life, gaining complexity when she herself was behind bars for her revolutionary work. While detained in her prison cell during her final imprisonment, Rosa slaved over a translation of Vladimir

Korolenko's autobiographical novel *A History of My Contemporary*, to which she supplied the introduction. The contradictions and misunderstandings she identifies in Korolenko's work and its reception give us insight into her own approach to the study of great (wo)men's lives and times. Luxemburg was first and foremost a freethinker and advocate of the right to dissent, to unpack social relations in order to bring justice into the world, and her writing collapses boundaries between the past, present and future. Rosa's analysis is entrenched in its own time, yet learns lessons from the past. About the change in Russian literature, she writes:

> That attitude toward society which enables one to be free of gnawing self-analysis and inner discord and considers 'God-willed conditions' as something elemental, accepting the acts of history as a sort of divine fate, is compatible with the most varied political and social systems. In fact it is found even under modern conditions and was especially characteristic of German society throughout the world war.[5]

This gives us a glimpse into Luxemburg's own interpretation of her times. She discusses the spirit of the new Russian literature as the 'struggle against darkness, ignorance, and oppression. With desperate strength it shook the social and political chains, bruised itself sore against them, and paid for the struggle in blood.'[6] Less than a year after writing those lines, she paid a price in blood in one of the most gruelling moments in the history of social democracy, a moment that gave way to the darkest period Germany has ever known. And yet, the life of Rosa Luxemburg is a story of resilience, integrity and love for the world. She once wrote how the writer Turgenev had enjoyed for the first time fully hearing the sound of a lark singing when 'he was somewhere near Berlin. This casual remark seems very characteristic. Larks warble in Russia no less beautifully than in Germany.'[7] Rosa Luxemburg worked towards a world in which one and all can enjoy the song of the lark equally, wherever and whoever they are.

Rosa Luxemburg had an extraordinary perception of history and its significance to our thinking about and ability to understand the world. She made great strides in her writing – whether she was right or wrong; her errors are as significant as her predictions, and are as telling about her life and works. The writing left by Rosa Luxemburg is still today being discovered and rediscovered. This book focuses on introducing the reader to her key texts and lesser-known works.

Luxemburg's writing on the concept of the masses, which appears often in her works, is intimately linked to her understanding of history. The concept is not analytically identical to Marx's proletarian class (which of course appears in her writing as well). The masses, those who move history towards revolution, remain vague and unproblematized in her archive. This book is intended to be a helpful vista into the force as well as the limitations of Luxemburg's work; her understanding and belief of the momentum of history, and the open-endedness of processes (even when read through a detailed historical-materialist lens), meant that our ability to predict events was limited. In the end, Rosa's understanding of the fact that history has its own force that can never be captured perfectly, occurring through multitudinous events, always in flux, is helpful as a way to understand some processes that constructed her own life, and the events of history that brought her to an untimely end.

Rosa's complex personality and rich legacy provide a challenge for the contemporary reader. This book is organized as a chronological narrative, but also according to the many spheres in which she agitated and worked. The first chapter is devoted to her life in Poland; the second to her work in the most significant international organization of her time, the Second International, and the first Russian Revolution; the third shows her most creative years in writing alongside her high-spirited engagement with the politics of the Social Democratic Party in Germany; the fourth looks at her life and work in prison; while the fifth focuses on the two parallel, yet hugely different, revolutions as examined by Luxemburg: the Russian Revolution of 1917 and the German Revolution of 1918–19.

This work, which follows in Luxemburg's footsteps, aims to present her texts and ideas in a clear and accessible manner, while understanding them better by unravelling her extraordinary life, and showing both continuity and difference within her archive. Whereas the breadth of this biography cannot encompass all of her work, this book does try to locate her writings in correspondence with each other and within their historical and biographical context. As she herself remarked: 'by itself every book is something terribly unapproachable.'[8] Rosa Luxemburg wrote four full-length book manuscripts, and many essays and speeches; some of the key texts are discussed here to show the development of her thinking and actions. This book examines, in the spirit of her historically attentive research itself, which ideas have survived the march of time since she left the world, and which have been proven wrong by history.

Too often we see works that focus on men's professional accomplishments, or, conversely, women's private lives. This book is thus explicitly a feminist work. Men and women are products of the private and the public; the following chapters aim to unravel the public Frau Dr Luxemburg as well as the private Rosa, while being attentive to contradictions within both those narratives. In a letter to her friend and secretary Mathilde Jacob, she wrote,

> can you tell me why I live constantly like this, without any inclination to do so? I would like to paint and live on a little plot of land where I can feed and love the animals.

> I would like to study natural science but above all else to live peacefully and on my own, not in this eternal whirlwind.[9]

And yet Rosa always resided at the heart of the storm.

We are all complex human beings, products of every relationship and challenge. Rosa Luxemburg offered some advice that has inspired the writing of this book, as I hope it will inspire those reading it:

> I believe people need to live in the subject matter fully and experience it every time, every day, with every article they write, and then words will be found that are fresh, that come from the heart and go to the heart, instead of [just repeating] the old familiar phrases. But people are so used to one or another truth or verity that they prattle or spout about the deepest and greatest subjects as though they were mumbling a Pater Noster. I hereby vow never to forget when I'm writing to be inspired again, on each occasion, about what I'm writing and to go inside myself for that.[10]

Let us follow then in the steps of Rosa Luxemburg, fully and completely.

In 1917, a woman takes an evening walk in a prison yard. Her steps are measured; her eyes attentive. Suddenly, she notices buffaloes pulling a wagon filled with shirts tainted by blood and shredded uniforms sent back from the front. The whole crux of evil in the world is elucidated and enveloped in this moment of one woman staring into a buffalo's eyes. Women, men and animals are pitted against each other, and taught that violence and bloodshed are necessarily the way of the world. Yet the essence of justice and empathy is carried in the eyes of the woman meeting the eyes of the animal. Resistance lies not only in throwing one's body on the altar, but in the quest to love and understand in the face of senseless violence. When war and bloodshed are the backdrop, one small woman, walking with a limp, staring into the buffalo's eyes, is proof that humanity triumphs in dark times.

1

A Clap of Thunder

Rozalia (Rosalie, Rosa) Lukensburg (Luxemburg) entered the world as a Jewish Polish citizen of the Russian empire on 5 March 1871 in the small town of Zamość. She was the youngest to join the Luxemburg family after Anna (born 1854), Mikolaj (1855), Maximilian (1860) and Jozef (1866).

The Luxemburgs were a middle-class Jewish Polish family. Jews in the Russian empire were twice oppressed: once as imperialist subjects, then as victims of religious discrimination, excluded from the minimal civil rights that even their fellow Poles had.[1] They were committed to the values of the Haskalah movement, a Jewish enlightenment movement that sprung out of Central and Western Europe between the 1770s and 1880s, as well as to the Continental culture that would be Rosa's intellectual cradle. The Luxemburg family was friendly with another famous descendant of Zamość, the Yiddish author Isaac Lieb Peretz.[2] The family was involved in both gentile and Jewish life. Rosa's paternal grandfather, Abraham Luxemburg, was a successful timber merchant. Edward Luxemburg was born to Abraham on 17 December 1803. His Hebrew name was Elisha, and later he adopted the name Eliasz. Edward was raised with both Polish and Yiddish, and attended school in Germany, where he embraced progressive ideas and in particular a passion for West European literature.[3] Rosa's mother, Lina Lowenstein, was the daughter of a rabbi. Lina was deeply religious and a passionate advocate of art, but the Luxemburg household was an assimilated

Jewish home, with great sensitivity to culture. Rosa recalled in 1917 that her mother considered Schiller to be the second-highest source of wisdom, after the Bible.[4]

Eliasz strove to give his children better possibilities in the world. The Luxemburg home was filled with poetry, which became intertwined with the narrative of Rosa's life. Rosa herself preferred Goethe throughout her life; yet the Jewish strands of her home never left her. She was also a dedicated reader of the Polish poet Adam Mickiewicz, part and parcel of her Polish-Jewish household. At age 47, she wrote about the Russian author Vladimir Korolenko, 'my soul, of a threefold nationality, has at last found a home – and this above all in the literature of Russia.'[5] She writes:

> descended at once from Poland, Russia and the Ukraine, Korolenko had to bear, even as a child, the brunt of the three 'nationalisms', each one expecting him to 'hate or persecute someone or other'. He failed these exceptions, however, thanks to his healthy common sense . . . And thus, from the conflict of three nationalities that fought in his native land of Volhynia, he made his escape into humanitarianism.[6]

Rosa's early days were of internationalism and from the womb her focus on humanity as a whole is echoed in the paths she took as she wrote and walked.

The Luxemburg family moved to Warsaw when Rosa was two and a half years old, as Eliasz was searching for a better education for his children.[7] Shortly after arriving in Warsaw, Rosa developed a disease of the hip,[8] which was wrongly diagnosed and left her with a limp that would remain a lifelong condition.[9] Her intellectual excellence as well as her disability made the Luxemburg siblings protective of her, and she quickly became the family's favourite. Rosa's sister Anna had suffered the same hip disease as Rosa and was not perceived as suitable for a life as married woman and mother

Rosa Luxemburg aged four, in 1875.

due to her disability. She stayed with her parents while Rosa was granted freedom to explore her destiny along a remarkably different path. A warm disposition combined with sharp intellectual wit allowed her to quickly win over the affections of all who met her. Her brilliant mind shone early; it is believed that at the age of nine she was already translating German poems and prose into Polish.[10]

The use of the Polish language was not allowed in the school Rosa attended in Warsaw.[11] At school, the combination of the repression of culture and absolutist rule created hotbeds of resistance. Young Rosa, with a feisty and disobedient nature, soon became a leader in those circles. In 1884, at the age of thirteen, she wrote a poem at the occasion of the visit of the German emperor William I to Warsaw:

> Finally we shall see you, mighty man of the West,
> At least, if you deign to enter our local park,
> Since I don't visit at your courts.
> Your honours mean nothing to me, I would have you know,
> But I would like to know what you're going to chatter about.
> With our 'royalty' you are supposed to be on intimate terms.
> In politics I'm still an innocent lamb,
> That's why I anyhow don't want to talk to you.
> Just one thing I want to say to you, dear William.
> Tell your wily fox Bismarck,
> For the sake of Europe, Emperor of the West,
> Tell him not to disgrace the pants of peace.[12]

A complete irreverence to authority combined with a sharp perception of the world accompanied Rosa from childhood. And this disregard for authority and ceaseless questioning of order went hand in hand with her deep engagement with humanity – as a concept and in practice. Rosa recalled waking up one day before her father when everything was still asleep; a cat crept by on its

Rosa about twelve years old, possibly a photo taken to commemorate her Bat Mitzvah.

soft paws across the courtyard, a pair of sparrows were having a fight with a lot of cheeky chirping, and long, tall Antoni in his short sheepskin jacket, which he wore summer and winter, stood by the pump with both hands and chin resting on the handle of his broom, deep reflection etched on his sleepy, unwashed face.

She recounts how Antoni, a man of 'higher aspirations' to whom she gave books, but who was apparently a caretaker around the Luxemburg household, was guided by a higher interest in arts and letters – he loved letters in and for themselves. 'Back then I firmly believed the "life", that is "real life", was somewhere far away, off beyond the rooftops. Ever since then I've been chasing after it. But it is still hiding beyond one rooftop or another.'[13] For Rosa humanity and nature were always linked; she delved into the core of the matter she investigated, whether that was herself or another natural being she was studying. And whereas 'life' could be far away, she would never really stop from trying to chase it. One particular photo of Rosa as a child reveals deep, warm eyes, a confident gaze that warmed the hearts of others and an assured posture. She would never suffer fools gladly. The young Rosa Luxemburg displayed some characteristics that would be part of the older Rosa's psyche in later life; strong-headed, extremely empathic, extraordinarily intelligent, with a fierce sharpness alongside immeasurable emotional depth, teenage Rosa showed her commitment to justice early. She had a fiery temperament, and would love and hate with the same passion; her vivid eyes and mischievous smile would accompany her throughout her life.

In the year of Rosa's birth, 1871, Warsaw's Jews experienced one of the worst pogroms in Poland's history. Anti-Jewish violence was prevalent in the Russian empire of the nineteenth century, yet its surge in 1881–2 was a watershed moment for both imperial policy and Jewish response. Rosa's childhood was at a time of escalating tensions between Poles, Russians and Jews. Rosa was homeschooled by her mother, Lena, until she was nine. Her multilingual childhood enabled her to acquire further languages. As an adult Luxemburg spoke Polish, Yiddish, Russian, German, English and French, and often undertook work in translation in addition to her own writing.[14]

There were quotas for Jews in educational institutions, and discrimination and oppression continued even if they did manage to be accepted. Despite being top of her high-school class Rosa did not receive the distinction she deserved – Jews were not awarded these prizes. In 1887/8, Rosa joined her first ever political organization, the Proletariat Party,[15] which stood against strands of Polish independence gaining prevalence at that time; as stated in a party pamphlet, 'the Polish proletariat is completely separate from the privileged classes and enters the struggle as an independent class, distinct in its economic, political and moral undertakings.'[16] In 1883–4 the main activists of the party were arrested, and in 1886 many were either in prison or executed. Rosa was fifteen and already highly involved in her homeland's politics when four executions of central revolutionaries in the party were carried out.[17] The party later changed its name to the Second Proletariat. In 1903, in 'In Memory of the Proletarian Party', she wrote about the first political organization she had joined, seventeen years earlier, and in it she recounted the emphasis on education of the masses: even if their final goal was far from achieved, education nonetheless helped to galvanize them into action.[18] It was in this party that Rosa's own political education commenced. The death of the martyred politicians urged Rosa to acknowledge the high price human beings may pay for dissent:

> Men who stood on such a high intellectual plane as those four, who met death for an idea with heads held high, and who in dying encouraged and inflamed the living, are doubtless not the exclusive property of any particular party, group, or sect. They belong in the pantheon of all mankind, and anyone to whom the idea of freedom, no matter what its content or form, is truly precious should embrace them as kindred spirits and honor their memory.[19]

From childhood she would be sensitive to the cause of fighting for the right to think differently, including within socialist circles themselves.

In 1889 an unusual shipment crossed the border to Switzerland. Rosa was hidden in a peasant's cart, disguised by straw, travelling away from her place of birth. This was the first political move – of many to come – for the now exiled Rosa Luxemburg. She was smuggled abroad with the aid of her friend and mentor Marcin Kasprzak.[20]

Rosa took rooms in Zurich towards the end of 1889 in 77 Universitätstrasse.[21] While spending time in her rooms there, she loved glimpsing out the windows to the famous Lake Zurich and the winding path towards it, decorated in trees. She enrolled at the University of Zurich to study natural sciences and mathematics in 1890, but switched to law in 1892 – yet her interest in nature and natural sciences continued throughout her life.[22] She studied formally under Professor Julius Wolf, Professor Vogt, Professor Treichler and Professor Fleiner. Of all those names the most significant is Wolf. The relationship between young Rosa and Professor Wolf is telling of her unequivocal dismissal of all authority. Rosa was already famous in her circles for her sharp tongue and outstanding intellect. In classes her peers and friends would ask difficult questions, and young Rosa Luxemburg would argue back with confidence, well versed in the latest critical and cultural commentaries – even more so, perhaps, than her professor. Professor Wolf later acknowledged that 'she came to me from Poland already as a thorough Marxist.'[23]

The nineteenth century saw a surge in the opening of educational facilities to women. Rosa's enrolment in higher education was an example of these new paths for women. The campaign for higher education was part of the bourgeois women's campaign in the 1880s, though the process was incremental and differed in its pace around the world. In 1877 Helen Magill White was the first woman to be awarded a doctorate in the United States. In Sweden, Ellen Fries received her PhD in 1883. In France, Dorothea Klumpke was awarded a doctorate in sciences in 1893. In Germany, women were admitted to higher education on the same terms as men in the different states between 1900 and 1909.[24]

At the height of her student days, in 1893, at the age of 22, Rosa co-founded with Leo Jogiches the first political organization in her life, alongside leading members of the Polish Left: Adolf Warski, Julian Marchlewski, Feliz Dzerzhinki, Karl Solbelson, Jakob Furstenberg and Stanislaw Pestkowski. The Social Democratic Party of Poland and Lithuania (SDKPiL) was an illegal organization whose paper, *Sprawa Robotnicza* (Workers' Cause), was published in Paris. Its *raison d'être* was opposing the claims for Polish nationalism that were backed by the Polish Socialist Party (PPS). SDKPiL was a group of young people in which many worked as equals in its early years.[25] Perhaps this was an omen for a woman who would always champion socialist democracy with equality of speech and action. During her time in Zurich she came across some of the most well-known names in revolutionary circles, including Pavel Akselrod, Parvus Helphand and Vera Zasulich.[26]

Rosa's revolutionary practice was also enunciated in writing. She progressed swiftly from her undergraduate degree to a doctorate, working hard on a thesis that became her first book-length manuscript. *The Industrial Development of Poland* (1898) contains some of the early threads that would weave into Luxemburg's entire life and career. Her dissertation, written in German, was based on an extensive amount of literature and sources in several languages, exemplifying a thorough internationalist approach.[27]

The writing style of the work is clear and forceful, bringing together economic discussions with social-political imaginaries. Luxemburg's internationalism is the theme and the crux of this work; although she focuses on the relationship between Poland and the Russian empire, there is analysis of other economies, from the U.S. to Britain, and countries in the Orient. Though Marx is only mentioned by name once, this is clearly a work based in historical materialism.[28] The argument of the piece is elucidated clearly and forcefully throughout. The Polish bourgeoisie are more inclined to be aligned with fellow bourgeoisie than their own nationals. This claim, which Luxemburg establishes in data gathered from various sources, is posed directly in opposition to Marx's support of Polish nationalism. Marx and Engels focused attention on Russia, seeing it as crucial for political progress in the West after 1848.[29] Luxemburg showed that Poland, between the years 1820 and 1850, grew into a disproportionate economic power within the Russian empire. Moving into a national Poland, Luxemburg argues, would be a regression into pre-capitalist times. Moreover, Luxemburg claims that Polish independence is not only reactionary and counter-revolutionary; it goes against the march of history and will return the Poles into the hands of the retrograde gentry.[30] Luxemburg placed much faith in the revolutionary power of Russia.

She highlights that it was between the years 1850 and 1870 that most of the transition into large-scale industry occurred. She notes several reasons for this: first, the abolition of the customs barrier between Russia and Poland; second, the creation of railways between Russia and Poland, and third, abolition of serfdom in Russia and Poland in the 1860s and the emancipation of the peasants. Luxemburg illuminated the relationship between Moscow and Łódź – the Russian empire and its Polish subject. Luxemburg contextualized her argument within trends in imperialistic Russian interests in the Orient. She ends the text forcefully:

> we believe that the Russian government, the Polish bourgeoisie and the Polish nationalists have all equally been struck with blindness, and that the capitalist fusion process between Poland and Russia has also a dialectical side that they have completely overlooked. That process is bringing to fruition in its own womb the moment when the development of capitalism in Russia will be thrown into contradiction with the absolutist form of government, and then tsarist rule will be brought down by its own works . . . the capitalist fusing of Poland and Russia is engendering as its end result that which has been overlooked to the same degree by the Russian government, the Polish bourgeoisie and the Polish

nationalists: the union of the Polish and Russian proletariat as the future receiver in the bankruptcy of the rule of the Russian Tsarism, and then the rule of Polish Russian capital.[31]

Here one of Luxemburg's foci becomes clear: the Polish question and her opposition to calls for Polish nationalism from both the Left and Right. Like many of her writings, Luxemburg ends on a note of agitation; her writing ends with a call for action, looking towards a new future.

Luxemburg's judgement in this piece as well as her arguments about the national question did not prove correct against the long arc of history. Neither did her predictions that Finland would not achieve political independence in relation to its ties with the Russian empire (Finland and Poland both gained independence in 1917). Historical developments have shown that the claim that Polish independence would become impractical did not hold. And yet, this first full-length work by Luxemburg is telling not only of her weaknesses but her strengths. Most of all, it is revealing of a young woman speaking from the margins who was never afraid to dissent. The dissertation contained the seeds of her developing work and was published a year after she had submitted it on 12 March 1897, a week after her 26th birthday. It was favourably and enthusiastically reviewed by leading thinkers of her time in the international press; despite the fact Luxemburg would make her formal intervention on the international stage a year later through her debate with Eduard Bernstein, she was already established as an important Marxist thinker.[32]

In Zurich, young Rosa's life was undergoing revolutions of various kinds. Leo Jogiches was a dark, handsome stranger. Four years older than Rosa, he was born in Vilnius, now part of Lithuania, to wealthy Jewish parents. Rosa and Leo had met in 1890 when they were both students and organized in the same circles. He was a natural and charismatic speaker; she was a talented writer rays pushed him (mostly unsuccessfully) to write more.

elationship became, and continued to be, a commitment to a snared cause alongside a deeply passionate love affair. Rosa's multinational cultural interests enabled her to accommodate new cultures and appeal to new audiences more easily than strong-headed Leo. Jogiches had inherited wealth which supported their revolutionary lifestyle, although he also kept a working-class job to efface his material conditions. Their bond of passion and urge for justice created the grounds for a lifelong collaboration.

Rosa's letters to Leo show the depth of her self-awareness in a relationship that knew dramatic ups and downs, but was fuelled by erotic passion and intellectual fire: 'I am writing partly because I have the stupid habit of saying what I feel, and partly because I want you to be *au Courant* with how things are between us.'[33] Rosa's self-revelation is intertwined with the depth of this relationship. The tension between her passion for Leo, her dreaming of a settled, bourgeois life, and the spark of revolution marching her onwards seems to be not easily reconciled: 'Of course, I'd be happy to have you in my *home* instead of being your guest. Of course, I'd like you to see how I live, and I'd like you to see everything besides.'[34] (Rosa referred to herself as 'your wife' after they had first made love.) Her desire and the explorative sexuality that spilled from her letters reveal her sensuality; she was as open-hearted as she was intellectually fierce.

Leo and Rosa's life together trod the line between the revolutionary – their shared cause embedded in the changing times – and routine. Neither of them was able to reconcile this tension. Rosa wrote, 'My entire soul is filled with you, and it embraces you . . . I want to love you. I want the same gentle, trusting, ideal atmosphere to exist between us as existed back then.'[35] The struggle to find a sphere for herself to share with her lover, while living a life centred on collective action, would haunt women activists long after Rosa, and yet her articulation of this contradiction is striking.

Leo Jogiches, Rosa's first lover. She never managed to reconcile her revolutionary spirit with living in a patriarchal world.

The depth of their union in her soul is revealed later in the letter: 'Without meaning to, I observe everything with your eyes and take pains with every little thing and arrange it as you would, the way that would please you. When will you finally see it?!'[36] Rosa loved children and wanted a child: 'we'll be in an empty house forever . . . more and more often I seriously think of adopting a child. This would be possible only if we've a regular income and sufficient means. Will I be too old then to raise a child?'[37] Rosa was truly *sui generis*, a radical new soul trying to carve a space for her own voice to grow and be heard in a swiftly changing world. Leo never understood that struggle, as she herself was well aware:

You, my dear, often understand me too superficially. You think I'm always 'sulking' because you're going away or something like that. And you can't imagine that it hurts me deeply that for you our relationship is something totally external.[38]

Rosa was self-conscious of her appearance – she was unusually short; when she wrote to Leo to stay away from Paris, she exclaimed, 'And really, how many beautiful women are here! Really, all of them are beautiful, or at least they seem to be. No, under no circumstances will you come here! You stay in Zurich!'[39] Leo and Rosa lived together for some of their time in Zurich, fulfilling several of her aspirations for a settled family life, though always only fleetingly. Rosa never got the bourgeois home and family she had hungered for, a craving that stood in stark contradiction to her revolutionary spirit and consequent commitments.

As Rosa and Leo's love affair developed, so did her inimitable personality, as she herself began to understand her uniqueness in the world:

It's the form of writing that no longer satisfies me. In my 'soul' a totally new, original form is ripening that ignores all rules and conventions. It breaks them by the power of ideas and strong conviction. I want to affect people like a clap of thunder, to inflame their minds not by speechifying but with the breadth of my vision, the strength of my conviction, and the power of my expression.[40]

The self-awareness of this eternal outsider, always on unequal standing with others and yet demanding her voice be heard, was just one of the qualities developing within her that would remain all her life.

Rosa Luxemburg was self-consciously a woman, and a woman living in a patriarchal world. Yet her refusal to accept limitations or societal determinations on what is appropriate or right are most apparent in her earlier letters to Leo. For a historical materialist, sex cannot be treated in *fin de siècle* niceties; and it is in the embodied idioms of her letters to Leo that we see the dialectic of Rosa Luxemburg in the private as well as the public sphere. She explored with Leo the boundaries of freedom of the body as well as the mind, and learnt that her lack of freedom came as much from herself as from what Leo and their joint hatred of the 'bourgeois' inflicted upon them both. Her psyche and body were that of a woman; she could not transcend the patriarchy. Nonetheless, always guided by her unique sense of humour, she wrote to Leo: 'I have the accursed desire to be happy, and would be ready, day after day, to haggle with my little portion of happiness with the foolish obstinacy of a pigeon.'[41]

The world of politics never allowed Rosa to be free of contradictions and challenges and to simply dwell in happiness. One particular scandal unsettled the French and international Left from 1894. That year, a French Jewish officer, Alfred Dreyfus, was sentenced to life behind bars on Devil's Island off French Guiana as a consequence of, allegedly, communicating military secrets to German officials – the evidence, his supposed letter to the German officers, was found by a French spy ripped up at the Germany embassy of Paris. Dreyfus' insignia was torn in a public ceremony and he was paraded before a crowd shouting 'Death to Judas, death to the Jew'. The Dreyfus Affair would become synonymous with anti-Semitism and the scapegoating of Jews. Luxemburg supported Jean Jaurès' position in supporting Dreyfus, intervening in 1899. Like many Marxists of her time, she perceived anti-Semitism to be a consequence of the class struggle. She began by arguing that class struggle must be the prism for understanding each conflict and deciding on the right course of action:

As concerns the Dreyfus Affair in particular, the intervention of the proletariat in the case need not be justified either from on [*sic*] general point of view, on the subject of bourgeois conflicts, nor from the point of view of humanity. For in the Dreyfus case four social factors make themselves felt which give it the stamp of a question directly related to the class struggle. They are: militarism, chauvinism-nationalism, anti-Semitism, and clericalism.[42]

In this text, Rosa indicates that the person is simply part of the greater cause, as she continued to argue:

Properly speaking, the political importance of the Dreyfus Affair consists, for us, in that the affair gave the possibility of making a great movement, one which shook the entire country, the object of the class struggle; and in this way we spread, in a short amount of time, more socialist consciousness than we could have developed over many years by means of abstract propaganda for our principles.[43]

Here the debate is about tactics and methods; the figure of Dreyfus is completely jettisoned from the discussion. The analysis is very generalized and has little of the fingerprints of her own Jewishness. Instead it subsumes questions of anti-Semitism, and racism, within class struggle.

In 1901, in a work entitled *The Socialist Crisis in France*, comprising five essays originally published in *Die Neue Zeit* (The New Times), Luxemburg writes:

The outcome of the Dreyfus Affair was of decisive importance for the Jaurès group, whether they liked it or not. To play on this card, and this card only, had been their tactic for two full years. The Dreyfus Affair was the axis of all their politics. They described it as 'one of the greatest battles of the century, one of the greatest of human history!' To shrink from this great task of the working class would mean 'the worst abdication, the worst humiliation.'[44]

Rosa claimed elsewhere that religion was a private affair, and religion would be reinterpreted and allotted its proper place in society through socialism, like other forms of oppression:

> When one speaks of an anti-clerical policy of Socialism, it is evident that it is not intended to attack religious convictions from a Socialistic point of view. The religion of the masses will only completely disappear with the society of today, when man, instead of being dominated by the social process, will dominate it and consciously direct it. This sentiment grows less and less as the masses, educated by Socialism, begin to understand social evolution.[45]

Rosa was an atheist but proud of her Jewishness, and her life was an extended lesson on the implications of being Jewish and a woman in the public eye.[46]

She graduated on 1 May 1897, three months after submitting her doctoral thesis. The first ever woman to be admitted to any degree at the University of Zurich had been enrolled thirty years before in 1867. Rosa's professor had awarded her summa cum laude ('with highest honours') but the faculty heads decided this was too much for a woman and so the grade was reduced.[47] Her family was immensely proud, and she was becoming better known in Marxist and revolutionary circles.[48] Rosa's next steps were already becoming clear. Rosa Luxemburg the revolutionary was already on the move, on her own, to the next big thing in the throbbing heart of international socialism: Berlin.

In order to be granted German citizenship Luxemburg married the son of an old friend, Gustav Lübeck, in Basel in mid-April

1898.[49] It was a marriage of convenience; there was no sentiment in the union. Rosa's eyes were firmly on the cause, and she arrived in Berlin in mid-May 1898. She arrived months before an election and began her involvement by agitating in Upper Silesia.[50] The socialist movement was large and well advanced compared to many other countries. She noted when flat-hunting in Berlin that some of the landlords were 'Philistines who surely would have fainted if the police asked about me (they've never seen a "Frau Doktor" before)'.[51] At less than thirty years old, and a Polish Jewess, Rosa ensured her rise to influence in international socialism was well planned. The Social Democratic Party of Germany (SPD) would be her next sphere of intervention, and would be a focus of her attention to last her entire lifetime; like many other journeys she would undertake, she embarked on this one on her own.

The SPD had a long history before Rosa was to march on to its centre stage. The General German Workers' Association and Social Democratic Workers' party merged in 1875 under the name Socialist Workers' Party of Germany (Sozialistische Arbeiterpartei Deutschlands, SAPD). The *Vorwärts* was SPD's newspaper. Catholics, socialists and Jews were often constructed as common enemies of the German nation. From 1878 to 1890, any grouping or meeting that aimed at spreading socialist principles was banned under the anti-socialist laws, but the party still gained support in elections. In 1890, when the ban was lifted and it could again present electoral lists, the party adopted its current name.

One of the most important figures in the SPD was Wilhelm Liebknecht, the 'soldier of the Revolution' and personal friend to Karl Marx. Many Jews were involved in the party when Rosa Luxemburg joined.[52] Rosa settled into her new environment fairly quickly, and already in 1898 was looking forward to hosting her sister Anna in her new home.[53] The Luxemburg family were busy in 1898, as Rosa wrote proudly of her brother Jozef being awarded a prize in a competition held by the Warsaw Medical Association, to which she commented, 'that made me very happy'; an article of his was even published in the *Berlin Medical Weekly*.[54]

The main movers and shakers of the SPD made Berlin a vibrant environment for the talk and action of socialism. Besides August Bebel and Liebknecht, there were other personalities to whom Rosa was introduced upon her arrival in Berlin who would become part of her new peer group through her engagement with the SPD. Karl and Luise Kautsky became personal friends early on. Karl Kautsky, co-founder of *Die Neue Zeit*, known as 'the Pope of Marxism' by friends and foes alike, was an early contact in Berlin. His wife Luise, a pioneering feminist, quickly became a trusted friend. Franz Mehring, historian of the SPD, was another prime personality of end-of-century socialist Berlin. In the city, Rosa met a woman who would become a lifelong ally and comrade-sister, Clara Zetkin, an activist and theorist in the social democratic women's movement, and a central figure in the working women's international movement. Last, Rosa met a fellow Jew, Eduard Bernstein, a self-educated writer and thinker. He was a personal friend of the Marx family and a significant student of Marx's collaborator Friedrich Engels.

Based on false assumptions that the financial boom of the 1890s showed the sustainability of capitalism, and appealing to change in the world as it was rather than preaching for a better future, Bernstein wrote a series of articles in the *Neue Zeit* that sparked the debate that marked the end of the nineteenth century in socialist discussions. Those articles then became his book *Evolutionary Socialism* (1907; originally published in German in 1899), which, as the title implies, removed the revolutionary component from socialist thinking, and the dialectic from the heart of socialism. The substitution of evolution with revolution comes to the crux of questions which still engage the Left today and which inspired Rosa Luxemburg's soaring critique *Social Reform or Revolution*, written in 1899 – does one concede to reforms, bettering the lives of the working class now, or does one work towards a radical overhaul of structures of society to offer dignity and humanity for all?

Rosa's confidence and integrity shone through in her narration of the writing process for this work, as stated in a letter to Leo:

> I have come to the same conclusion as you, that precisely the Bernstein question must be the 'great work' that I will have to write. Thank God that K. K. [Karl Kautsky], as he explained to me categorically and even showing surprise, has no intention of writing a pamphlet (only [something] in the *Neue Zeit*). The only other person who has such an intention is Parvus, but I have no apprehensions about him as a Competitor.

The self-assurance and motivation of this young woman, a complete outsider to well-established circles, steered her in her course for publication: 'After the pamphlet by Bernstein appears, another one opposing it will have every chance of success. So I will present this "series" as a reply to Ede [Bernstein] – that is, not now but immediately after his book appears.' The tactic is well argued and calculated. Rosa is ready to take the SPD by storm, while showing no doubt of what her reception will be; to present 'polemical twists and turns in such a way as to block or counter Bernstein's main arguments ahead of time – that would be offering food that is too refined [*zu feines Fressen*] for this audience. No one will give it value.'[55]

Social Reform or Revolution was Rosa Luxemburg's first major intervention in international radical circles. She was already known for her organizing and earlier book, yet she knew that this would be her breakthrough piece. The work, influenced by Marx's *Communist Manifesto* in form and content, is telling both in its narrative of her life, as well as the elements that will later grow in her thinking. It was her first major political work, and one of her most enduring. She herself rightly considered it the work by which she would earn

Luxemburg on an SPD picnic (second from the left), 1905, Berlin, her adopted new home. In 1919 she would write her last ever agitating words: '"Order reigns in Berlin!" You stupid lackeys! Your "order" is built on sand. Tomorrow the revolution will "raise up again clashing," and to your horror it will proclaim to the sound of trumpets: *I was, I am, I shall be!*'

her political spurs in the SPD, and force the old guard take her seriously.[56]

The argument of the work challenged Bernstein's points one by one and by so doing took down opportunism in theory and practice. In it, we can see the characteristics that would reappear throughout Rosa's works: the intertwining of political and economic analysis, the attention to historical subtlety, multilayered arguments touching upon various spheres of life, and, crucially, the interleaving of agitation for action in any piece of reflection. Agitation was central to her life's work. The style of *Social Reform or Revolution* reflects her self-assurance, dotted with humorous anecdotes, literary quips and creative use of language. Her mistakes remain for history to judge; her writing style here, in this nascent text already apparent, is unique.

Luxemburg starts by stating that both social reform and revolution are vital to her praxis and political programme. Struggle for reforms is a means; revolution is the goal. She swiftly claims that 'reform or revolution' is akin to Hamlet's crucial line 'to be or not to be?' Further, 'The focus is on the existence of social-democratic movement, never merely tactics.'[57] Luxemburg proceeds to challenge the idea that theoretical discussions are for intellectuals. The belief in revolution is anything but a lofty, detached ideal; it is the insistence that those who are oppressed can overthrow those structures that keep them chained and constrained.

Bernstein's core argument was that the breakdown of capitalism was becoming extremely unlikely. Thus the general struggle of social democracy should focus on the improvement of the condition of the working class.[58] Luxemburg elucidates clearly the three fundamental assertions of capitalist development: first, the growing anarchy of capitalist economy; second, socialism as a system in which the future unfolds from the potentials of the present through the force of history; third, the growing organization and class consciousness of the proletariat.[59] Bernstein in fact removes the first of those assertions. This is a logical conundrum. 'Either revisionism is correct concerning the course of capitalist development, and therefore the socialist transformation of society becomes a utopia. Or socialism is not a utopia; and therefore the theory of the "means of adaptation" is false.'[60] The objective process of capitalism creates its own demise through the transformation of consciousness.

Luxemburg then outlines the political consequences of revisionism. Bernstein undermines the belief that both parliamentary struggle and the trade union movement can push the proletariat towards gaining power. Either of these processes, according to Bernstein, reduces capitalist exploitation in an objective way, or according to Rosa, the trade unions and parliamentary struggles create a subjective transformation.

These two positions, she argues, are diametrically opposed. The emphasis on the objective processes of capitalism creating its own crises and the incumbent seeds of its own demise does not exclude the focus on transformation of consciousness. The insistence on historical necessity does not eliminate the need for transforming subjectivity. Galvanizing the agency of the masses will lie at the heart of all of Rosa Luxemburg's work. At the same time, the careful and critical understanding of history allows for intervention in the correct moment. A critique that many Marxists would have to answer, which becomes central to Luxemburg's work, is articulated here clearly: the work of a Marxist theorist is always to both elucidate the progression of history as well as enable the transformation of the minds of those who make it.

Luxemburg pays attention to the fact that transformations such as universal suffrage are crucial to socialism. The analysis she presented in *Social Reform or Revolution* emphasized democracy as well as revolutionary Marxism. Luxemburg argued that there is no hope for developing a general law of the evolution of democracy outside of Marxist analysis.[61] The analytical consequence of this claim is profound, as it means the struggle not only insists on transformation of economic structures, the classical Marxist position, but rather separately needs to be attentive to democracy. In this text her argument is not honed, but the claim above is crucial for understanding Luxemburg's legacy.

> Democracy does not acquire greater chances of life in the measure that the working class renounces the struggle for its emancipation. On the contrary, democracy acquires greater chances of survival as the socialist movement becomes sufficiently strong to struggle against the reactionary consequences of world politics and the bourgeoisie desertion of democracy. He who would strengthen democracy must also want to strengthen and not weaken the socialist movement;

and with the renunciation of the struggle for socialism goes that of both the labor movement and democracy.[62]

She proceeds to the zenith of the argument:

> Legal reform and revolution are not different methods of historical progress that can be picked out at pleasure from the counter of history like one chooses hot or cold sausages. They are different moments in the development of class society which condition and complement each other, and at the same time exclude each other reciprocally.[63]

After her theoretical claim is assessed fully, Luxemburg proceeds to argue that every legal constitution is a result of a revolution – an overarching claim that has consequences both to the understanding of legal changes as well as to the concept of revolution. Luxemburg concludes: 'democracy is indispensable not because it renders superfluous the conquest of power by the proletariat but, on the contrary, because it renders the conquest of power both necessary as well as possible.'[64]

Democracy is necessary for the triumph of socialism, and the two are logically, ethically and politically intertwined. What Bernstein's theory lacks most profoundly, by comparison to Luxemburg's account, is the catalyst for action of the masses. It lacks a positive programme. This search for a positive programme underpins Luxemburg's work. *Social Reform or Revolution* focuses on collective power and poses Rosa's unique analysis of the form revolutionary democracy is to take in a moment of crisis. The conceptual centrality of the revolution as well as insistence on a dialectical method of understanding the world were central to her practice from this text on. The text itself is a well-honed piece of writing; it is vibrant, bursting with humorous notes and literary references, from Talmudic subtleties to Shakespeare's 'to be or not to be'.

Rosa was not the only one to take on Bernstein's debate, insisting on Marx's centring of revolution in theory and practice. Karl Kautsky also challenged Bernstein from within the SPD. Another response came much closer to home, from Marx's youngest daughter, Eleanor. By the time of the publication of Bernstein's articles Eleanor was a respected writer, editor and agitator in her own right, and her work stood at the centre of international socialism. Friedrich Engels was like a second father to her. Bernstein was a close friend. In a letter to her sister Laura she refers to Bernstein's articles as a wet blanket, and argues, echoing Rosa, that they are 'not exactly useful at the present moment'.[65] Eleanor suggested in 1896 that Bernstein's interpretation could be open to debate; Bernstein, 'in breathtakingly patronizing and sexist terms, refused'.[66] Bernstein, a dear friend to all of the Marx family, blew up in the face of any criticism. In response, Eleanor decided to edit and publish one of her father's 'admirable expositions', *Value, Price and Profit* (written in 1865), a lasting gem in Marxist legacy, not often attributed to this debate.

Rosa was to achieve worldwide recognition for her intervention in what became known as 'the revisionist debate'. In October 1898, to roaring applause, Rosa hit the last nail in her critique of revisionism:

And then the well-known statement [by Bernstein] in the *Neue Zeit*: 'The final goal, whatever it may be, is nothing to me: the movement is everything!' Anyone who says that does not stand for the necessity of seizing political power. You see that some comrades in the Party do not stand for the final goals of our movement, and that it is necessary to express that fact unambiguously. If ever it was necessary, now is the time. The blows of reaction shower on us like hail. This debate must answer the Kaiser's latest speech. Like the Roman Cato, we

Portrait of Rosa Luxemburg, n.d. She wrote in 1913: 'The whole development, the whole tendency of imperialism in the last decade leads the international working class to see more clearly and more tangibly that only the personal stepping forward of the broadest masses, their personal political action, mass demonstrations, and mass strikes which must sooner or later open into a period of revolutionary struggles for the power in the state, can give the correct answer of the proletariat to the immense oppression of imperialistic policy.'

must say sharply and clearly, 'In addition, I am of the opinion that this state must be destroyed.' The conquest of political power remains the final goal and that final goal remains the soul of the struggle. The working class cannot take the decadent position of the philosophers: 'The final goal is nothing to me, the movement is everything.' No, on the contrary, without relating the movement to the final goal, the movement as an end in itself is nothing to me, the final goal is everything.[67]

The final goal was only just appearing on the horizon, as Rosa Luxemburg, a clap of thunder, burst into the international socialist world.

2

Dress Rehearsal for the Revolution

Rosa Luxemburg made colossal strides not only in the SPD, but in the most crucial organization for revolutionary theory and practice in the early twentieth century, the Second International. September 1864 had marked the foundation of the International Workingmen's Association, now referenced as the First International, in London. A wide range of assorted radicals had come together alongside a then relatively unknown refugee journalist, Karl Marx. The First International became crucial for the development of Marx's legacy as well as socialism and radical thinking worldwide. By the time the International came to its end in 1876, Marx had already published his work *Capital*, which would become a core text for all radical thinkers following in his footsteps. Marx's famous dictum in his *Theses on Feuerbach* (published in 1888), 'the philosophers have only interpreted the world in various ways; the point, however, is to change it', meant that those who took Karl Marx's work to heart had to advance it in both theory and practice. For that, an international organization was crucial. As Marx commented on the International:

> It is not . . . a mere improvement that is contemplated, but nothing less than a regeneration, and that not of one nation only, but of mankind. This is certainly the most extensive aim ever contemplated by any institution, with the exception, perhaps, of the Christian Church. To be brief, this is the programme of the International Workingmen's Association.[1]

The Second International formed out of a collaboration between German social democrats and Belgian socialists in Chur, Switzerland, in October 1881. Whereas the first international was comprised mostly of trade unionists and individuals, the Second International was an organization of political parties with an elected leadership. In 1886 in Paris an International Labour Congress showed signs of progress towards a new International with parties representing Italy, Spain, Holland, Belgium, Great Britain, the Scandinavian countries, France, the United States and more. The year 1889 saw two congresses in Paris owing to an internal split in the movement. Divides and divergences are just as crucial to understanding the development of theory and practice of the Second International as its call for unity. The first congress was supported by most of the French and the second by Engels (though he did not attend) and the German Socialists. The 1889 congress also featured a speech from Clara Zetkin that would become fundamental for socialist-feminism generally and within the International specifically; it was translated by Eleanor Marx, who herself spoke of socialist feminism at this Congress.[2] Two years later, Eleanor Marx wrote a report on the congress of 1891, a congress that signalled the unification of both factions. Eleanor was a crucial activist and theorist in the Second International; taking forward her father's legacy, she galvanized as well as chronicled discussions on the eight-hour work day and trade unionism. Her written report of this International concluded with a call to arms: 'Long live the International Solidarity of the Working Class Movement!'[3]

The next congress was held in 1893 in Zurich, and was attended by some of socialism's biggest names, including Engels – who was elected honorary president – August Bebel, Wilhelm Liebknecht, Karl Kautsky and Clara Zetkin.[4] That year was a busy one for the doctoral student Rosa Luxemburg. She co-founded the Social Democracy of the Kingdom of Poland (SDKP), and made the stride into international organizing. Rosa was rejected as an official delegate of another Polish party, the Polish Socialist Party (PPS), founded a year before, which argued for independence for Poland, unlike the internationalist SDKP. She was allowed to make a report to the congress on the political landscape of Russian Poland.[5]

Emile Vandervelde, the Belgian socialist leader, described the scene:

> Rosa, 23 years old at the time, was quite unknown outside one or two socialist groups in Germany and Poland . . . but her opponents had their hands full to hold their ground against her . . . I can see her now: how she sprang from among the delegates and jumped unto a chair to make herself better heard. Small, delicate and dainty in a summer dress which cleverly concealed her physical defects, she advocated her cause with such magnetism in her eyes and with such fiery words that she enthralled and won over the great majority of the congress, who raised their hands in favor of the acceptance of her mandate.[6]

A portrait of Rosa Luxemburg from 1893 shows her with short hair, probably self-cut, staring intently at the camera. Thus Rosa makes her fiery debut on the stage of the Second International. Eleanor Marx, who was central to the Second International from its inception, herself noted with approval young comrade Luxemburg.[7]

The secretary of the 1893 congress was Rosa's acquaintance Robert Seidel, whose wife, Mathilde, was also a friend. The congress furthered several agendas, but it ascertained that the eight-hour day would be declared the most important preliminary step towards the ultimate emancipation of the working class from the yoke of capital, and the most important measure for bettering their conditions.[8] May Day, or International Workers' Day, demonstrations were to be focused around the eight-hour day and other themes that bound international socialist organizations.

Rosa with short hair, which she probably cut herself, *c*. 1893, when she first attended the Second International.

In a letter to the Russian revolutionary, and a leader in the League of Russian Social-Democracy Abroad, Boris Krichevsky, written several months after the congress and which begins with a spirited 'worthy comrade!', Rosa reflected on the initial responses she received from the German labour movement; Wilhelm Liebknecht, the founder of the SPD, referred to her as *Genosse* – a male version of comrade. Rosa learnt that all comrades were not the same: 'By the way, I don't know why he addresses me as a man, calling me Genosse (after all, I did sign with my first name), rather than feminine "genossin".'[9] Rosa was always aware of the difference between her and her male comrades. She saw herself as equal, and yet the difference to them was apparent.

In 1896, a year after Engels's death, the International met in London over two sittings. The congress decided to finally exclude anarchists completely, and allowed more and more reformists to join its ranks, expanding to the Right. The French delegates Alexandre Millerand and Jean Jaurès, elected as bourgeois radicals and joining socialists to form a parliamentary fraction, also attended the congress. Auguste Marie Joseph Jean Léon Jaurès was the leader of the French Socialist Party. Never a Marxist, but a socialist, he was nonetheless appreciated by Luxemburg. Jaurès was the author of *A Socialist History of the French Revolution* (1901), an inquiry on political action that contained a frank recognition of the principles and objectives of revolutionary socialism. Whereas some pacifist enquiries – the calling for a resistance to the rise of militarism, and the 1896 peace demonstration in Hyde Park – boasted the congress's biggest names, a French proposal to respond to war with a general strike received no support. The tension between revolutionary socialism in ethos and its descent towards reformism in practice became enshrined in the International. The strategic contradictions behind the dictum 'workers of the world, unite!' and internationalism as a doctrine encompassing different areas and countries were expressed in central debates.

The 1896 congress was a significant moment for Rosa, because she was finally attending as a fully recognized delegate. The Galician Polish leader Ignacy Daszynski, however, accused her of being a police spy, there to disrupt the Polish movement.[10] Thus Rosa Luxemburg entered the Second International as both famous and infamous, with her sleeves rolled up and ready for a fight. The Polish question had returned to the congress following an article published simultaneously in the *Sprawa Robotnicza* and the Italian newspaper *Critica Sociale*. Luxemburg herself took on two central arguments regarding Polish independence. First was the belief that

Polish socialists were able to carry out their own programme, and that their accomplishments would be crucial to bringing forth the demise of the Russian empire – a position she had shared with her opponents on this question. Luxemburg refuted this, contending that Poland was not crucial to the strength of the Russian empire, and even if it gained independence it would be incidental to the empire, which would inevitably remain strong. Second, she argued that any Polish rebellions would be boldly suppressed – and the international proletariat was in a position to offer nothing but empathy to the Polish proletariat. Luxemburg argued that there would be a slippery slope effect: if Poland pursued independence, what would stop Alsace-Lorraine, Ireland or Czechoslovakia from also seeking it? And here we see the crux of Luxemburg's ideological resistance to the programme of independence of her own people, supported by the majority of Marxists worldwide. The internationalist Rosa Luxemburg feared that this demand – seen both in her time and in hindsight as a crucial bulwark against the Russian empire – would create a sweeping wave of nationalism.[11]

The Polish question is a central issue in which history has proven Luxemburg wrong. She understood well the role of national cultures, specifically with regard to her own situation, an exile at a very young age. In a letter to Leo, Rosa wrote, 'the only strong impression is the one I've already written to you about – the fields of grain and the Polish landscape.'[12] In another letter she wrote to Leo that she could cite many other truly Polish proverbs, 'only I'm afraid this pure Polish is precisely something you won't understand.'[13] The woman of three homelands retained an emotional connection to Poland, yet never wavered from arguing against Polish independence, a problematic position from tactical, ideological and theoretical points of view.

And yet, Rosa entered the Second International from a position opposed to that advocated by Marx and Engels themselves. A democratic Poland, according to Marx, would aid in separating

Germany from Russia, thus creating more opportunities for revolution, as well as help anti-Russian agitation.[14] Rosa, however, did not accept this position. Moreover, she objected to socialist patriots like Bernstein who believed in combining social and national questions.[15] Indeed, Rosa's battle against reformism was intertwined with the battle against nationalism.[16] In her zeal, she overestimated the revolutionary potential within Russia,[17] but nevertheless Rosa's emphasis on the final goal was connected accordingly with her emphasis on internationalism.[18] Rosa assumed that nation-states are a by-product of capitalism, and hence concluded that all appendages of nationalism were bourgeois constructs.[19] There are interesting parallels between Rosa's positions on women's rights and national self-determination:

> The duty of the class party of the proletariat to protest and resist national oppression arises not from any special 'right of nations,' just as, for example, its striving for the social and political equality of sexes does not at all result from any special 'rights of women' which the movement of bourgeois emancipationists refers to. This duty arises solely from the general opposition to the class regime and to every form of social inequality and social domination, in a word, from the basic position of socialism.[20]

Any conception of rights, including a lifelong commitment to universal suffrage, arises solely from social-economic rights and liberties, and for Rosa a commitment to national rights stood in irreconcilable tension to the class struggle.

The new century brought many changes to the infamous Rosa, now Dr Luxemburg. During the time that she was swiftly rising within the ranks of the Second International, Rosa lost both of her parents, neither of whom lived to see her turn thirty years old. Lina Lowenstein died in September 1897; Eliasz died in September 1900. Rosa was, moreover, away from Poland. In a letter to Leo in

1905 she reflected: 'I pulled out the box with the last letters from Mama and Papa and the letters from Andzia and Jozio from that same time. I read through them all, and had to cry so hard that my eyes got completely swollen and I went to sleep with a huge wish never to wake up again.'[21] Rosa bemoaned the demands of the cause that pushed her to answer letters belatedly, and yet her love for her family never ceased. Rosa was close to her siblings, although the dangerous, outlying sister was someone risky to know.

With the arrival of the new century, the congress of 1900, held in Paris, signified the growth of urgency of certain questions that had been debated in past conventions and had since become pressing internationally. In terms of organizational structure, the most significant achievement of the 1900 congress was the foundation of the International Socialist Bureau, which aimed to profess socialism among the members' states and attempted to organize different labour movements with varying abilities and ethos. The centrality of reformism and revolution to the International highlighted the position that the SPD held within its ranks by then.

Two questions that were fundamental to Luxemburg's work were debated widely at the 1900 congress: that of imperialism and that of reformism versus revolution. The question of nationality and socialism, too, continued to stir the congress Underlying all these discussions was a continuous thread. Social democracy, as parties aligned with trade unions and mass labour movements, articulated questions of concessions towards winning votes and institutional power versus sustaining revolutionary, if also fringe, tendencies.

Luxemburg's work began to expand following her participation in the Internationals and the revolutionary tides at the start of the new century. An essay from 1902 shows Luxemburg moving towards a cohesive understanding of the world, bringing together internationalism, resistance to all opportunism and care for the world as a whole. Her essay 'Martinique' is a clear argument for environmentalism: it comments on the eruption of Mount Pelee volcano in May 1902, which caused nearly 30,000 human deaths, and is a stark condemnation of the opportunism of the tsar, Germany, Holland and England, who all suddenly showed the urge to extend a helping hand despite having had little or no interest in the island and its people before. Rosa's critique of English imperialism is bound together with her understanding of nature as transcending human abilities to control it:

> a volcano that is seething and boiling, whether you need it or not, will sweep the whole sanctimonious, blood-splattered culture from the face of the earth. And only on its ruins will the nations come together in true humanity, which will know but one deadly foe – blind, dead nature.[22]

At the same time in 1902 Rosa was carefully observing the general strike in Belgium, which had ended in defeat. Yet unlike her German comrades, Rosa blamed its failure on the conditions from which the strike arose, not the tactics of the strike itself.[23] She wrote about the Belgian strike in two articles in the *Neue Zeit*, and these would feed into her comprehensive analysis of strikes as central to revolutionary practice.

Rosa's ascent within the International assured her of her abilities as a public speaker on national and international platforms:

> You have no idea what good effect my attempts so far to speak at public meetings have had on me. I didn't have the slightest self-assurance in this respect, but had to take a chance and step out on the ice. Now I'm sure that in half a year's time I will be among the best of the party's speakers.[24]

She was becoming increasingly well known. In a letter of 1899 Rosa recounted a comment made by a comrade's wife after visiting her: 'RL is quite human.'[25] In 1900 she commented that the comrades had a different image of her, 'large and fat', and yet would exclaim when saying goodbye, 'we love you so!'[26] She recalls coming to speak in Reichenbach in 1902 and her audiences were amazed at how young she was.[27] In the same meeting she discussed pregnant women working in a factory alongside young men, to which her audience responded, 'those are mistaken moralistic notions! Can you imagine if our Luxemburg were pregnant here today while giving her lecture? Then I would like her even better!'[28] She reflected on this incident to Leo, and wondered whether she 'must make an effort to be pregnant the next time I go to Reichenbach'. She was asked by a young fellow, 'should he get married, even though present-day marriage is a perverse arrangement?' To which Rosa advised him that, indeed, he should, which happened to be the right response since his fiancée was 'in the condition that he likes very much'.[29]

Rosa was not what anyone expected her to be. The famed speaker and author of *Social Reform or Revolution*, whose portrait was held in adoration by expectant audiences, was always a woman in a man's world, anything but an agony aunt, and yet was expected to give advice to young men in a world in which gender relations were swiftly changing.

On 4 April 1903 Rosa received her formal divorce papers from Lubeck;[30] she had been living with Leo, who had arrived in Germany in 1900, and was organizing in Berlin. In this period a pattern emerges that would accompany her throughout her life: in her love and sex life she tested ideas of freedom, but never placed them on the public stage. She was fearless as a public advocate, and passionate in her emotional life, yet this aspect of her remained closed to her comrades. The struggles that accompany women in the public eye would haunt her all her life. It must be noted that two of Rosa's many contradictions were her financial dependency on Leo, apparent in her letters, and having maids. Rosa hated bourgeois feminism and its niceties, and yet strove to have a bourgeois lifestyle. Her excursions in Berlin to theatrical and musical events, often accompanied by friends or her niece Annie, a talented musician, must have created a different impression to Berliners from the now infamous 'red Rosa'.

In 1903 Rosa joined the International Socialist Bureau. In 1904 she claimed another victory; she represented both the SPD and SDKPiL at the Second International. In a photo from the 1904 International Congress we glimpse the developing role Rosa Luxemburg played in the Second International, as well as its contradictions. The photo presents a sea of dark suits. Throughout her life Rosa was a large bow among them.[31]

Rosa's commitment to Marxism and freedom, combined, was unwavering. In a text from 1903 commemorating the twentieth anniversary of the death of Karl Marx, she wrote:

> To speak with Engels, this final leap from the kingdom of necessity to the kingdom of freedom that only the socialist revolution will realise for society as a whole, already takes place *within the existing order* – in *social-democratic politics* ... Consequently, the part of Marxian theory that is most dangerous to the existing order of society will sooner or later be 'overcome'. But only *together* with the existing order of society.[32]

In a text from the same year the contradiction was elucidated clearly:

> Not until the working class has been liberated from its present conditions of existence will the Marxist method of research be socialized in conjunction with the other means of production, so that it can be fully utilized for the benefit of humanity at large, and so that it can be developed to the full measure of its functional capacity.[33]

At the Amsterdam 1904 Congress of the Second International, Rosa is easily recognizable wearing a large bow. 'Self-consciously a woman', Hannah Arendt wrote about her many years later.

In this period of Rosa's life we see the consolidation of the principles that became established across her writing and activism: the insistence on democracy and freedom within the Marxist tradition, sound belief in the forces of history to bring about the revolution, as well as unity between theory and action.

The year 1904 would signal a turning point in Rosa's life as well as within the history of the Second International. The International had accelerated many revolutionary processes in different countries and they were now on the verge of rupture. However, the winds of change were blowing east, where a debate around liberal bourgeois and socialist tactics was on the verge of making Russia the stage for the biggest revolutionary event of the early twentieth century.

In the same year, there would be the beginning of a dialogue and argument that would endure for Rosa's entire political life. Vladimir Ilyich Ulyanov, better known by the alias Lenin, was a political figure whose life and work would echo that of

Clara Zetkin and Rosa Luxemburg in a carriage with fellow socialists Pieter Jelles Troelstra and Emile Vandervelde, 1907.

Luxemburg's; their paths often intertwined and there was mutual respect between them. But Rosa's lifelong dispute with Lenin and the RSDLP (Russian Social Democratic Labour Party) which commenced with the revolution had ideological, structural and political dimensions. The question of organizational affiliation of the SDKPiL to the Russian RSDLP once again invoked Rosa's position on Polish independence. Her Russian comrades were of the classic Marxist position that affirmed Polish independence, much like the comrades in the Second International against whom she was battling. However, the Russians were advocates of revolutionary socialism and not reformism and so she was willing to collaborate with them despite this fundamental difference.[34]

This debate, however, teaches us certain lessons about Rosa's international position as well as her personality. She was able to be fierce in battle and yet warm in friendship with her opponents, as she was with Jaurès. Rosa once translated a work of Jaurès – when no one else was on hand to translate the French to German

– despite it being an accumulation of critiques against her own positions.[35] The debate between Lenin and Luxemburg would develop across the march of history, with both sides vindicated and refuted on different issues.

In her essay 'Organizational Questions of Russian Social Democracy' (published in the *Neue Zeit* in 1904), Rosa debated the question of grassroots organizations in democracy, within the specific context of Russia in comparison to Germany. In her response to Lenin's *One Step Forward, Two Steps Back*, also published in 1904 (subtitled *The Crisis in Our Party*), Luxemburg presents the tension between Leninist centralism and revolutionary Marxism crystallized in the action of the masses. She cites two principles in Lenin's centralism: first, the blind subordination, in the smallest detail, of all party organizers to the party centre, which alone thinks, guides and decides for all; second, the rigorous separation of the organized nucleus of revolutionaries from the party's social revolutionary surroundings. For Luxemburg social democracy is not joined by the proletariat; it itself is the proletariat. To realize social democratic centralism the working-class consciousness must be steeped in class struggle and workers should have the organizational method to develop their own political activity through direct influence on public life:

it is quite simply a misuse of the catchword simultaneously to characterize as 'discipline' two such opposing concepts as the lack of will and thought in a body with many arms and legs that moves mechanically to the baton and the voluntary coordination of the conscious political actions of a social stratum; such concepts as the blind obedience of an oppressed class and the organized rebellion of a class struggling for its emancipation. It is not through the discipline instilled in the proletariat by the capitalist state, with the straightforward transfer of the baton from the bourgeoisie to a social democratic

Committee, but only the defying and uprooting spirit of servile discipline that the proletarian can be educated for the new discipline, the voluntary self-discipline of social democracy.[36]

For Luxemburg a tension existed between democracy from below and the middle-class intellectual meant to be the vanguard of the working class; indeed she notes connections between opportunism and 'intellectuals'.[37] She argued that the best guarantee against opportunist intrigue and personal ambition was the independent revolutionary action of the proletariat, which would create workers who are responsible and self-reliant:

> the identification of the great popular mass with a goal that transcends the whole existing order and the identification of the day-to-day struggle with revolutionary upheaval constitute the dialectical contradiction of the social democracy movement which must, in the whole course of its development, work a way forward logically between the two pitfalls, between losing its mass character and abandoning its goal, between relapsing into sects and declining into a bourgeois reform movement.[38]

August Bebel and Rosa Luxemburg, 1904. Luxemburg was a target of sexism all her life, including from the author of the renowned work *Woman and Socialism*.

This commitment to dialectics – both as an interpretive method and a vista to see the world – and to historical materialism led Luxemburg to a subtle and robust interpretation of the fast changes of social and political configurations around her, derived out of her commitment to revolutionize the consciousness of the masses and induce them to action. Her critique was proven right by history, yet in this 'Organizational Questions of Russian Social Democracy' she drew as much on processes occurring around herself as she did on her subjects in Russia.

The concept of 'the masses' often appears in Luxemburg's work and it is as effective an analytical tool as it is vague. It is not clear exactly who 'the masses' are, hence it allows her to merge national analyses with a commitment to internationalism. Luxemburg uses the concept in a distinct way from Marx's concept of the proletariat. It also allows her, through its lack of analytical and conceptual clarity, to serve the overarching goal of spreading revolutionary socialism to the widest possible field. Action advances in a specific direction but without a proposed, known subject.

The dialectics of history brought dramatic changes to Rosa's life. She was imprisoned on 26 August 1904 for insulting the German emperor.[39] The child who once wrote rebellious poems was now being held accountable for her revolutionary actions on the public stage. She was accused of inciting the masses and was deemed exceptionally dangerous, to which she replied:

> Counsel for the prosecution holds that my excited tone deserved grave consideration. But surely the tone is a matter of individual temperament. Why, is it not possible that one may speak most excitedly, yet may present a strictly scientific conception, while, on the other hand, one may speak very quietly, yet present a very crude, unscientific, and alarming conception? And as far as my conception in regard to the

question of the General Strike is concerned, I hold the view that neither a revolution nor a great, serious General Strike can be produced or provoked in an artificial manner.

Nothing was ever cold analysis for Rosa Luxemburg; nor was it when she was re-presenting her argument to a public prosecutor. Passion fuelled her analysis and its delivery, and she was willing to take this accusation as a badge of honour.[40] As a political prisoner she was entitled to books, clothes and letters. Her letter to Luise and Karl Kautsky reveals her determination: 'for me the moral of the story is: that we have an incredible amount to do and above all an incredible amount to study, by which I mean the movement in the various countries.'[41]

Rosa read poetry from Schiller,[42] reflected, and kept to her daily routine of walks in the blazing sun.[43] She wrote to her friend Henriette Roland Holst three days after her release: 'in solitude I find myself again, and bring the "Polish economy" of my spiritual life into a well-ordered state of affairs.'[44] Rosa set herself a way of life:

One's guiding principle must be to achieve the greatest results with the smallest amount of effort. I am already following this principle here. To do everything calmly and lightly without getting myself worked up in the slightest way, and not to work too much on any one thing – that is my system.[45]

Luxemburg's psyche was always in movement: she was always attentive to multiple systems of oppression, and she explored issues both outside of herself and within, whether thinking of global capitalism or reaching inwards to examine her emotional depths. Her 'Polish economy', as she referred to her emotional life, was never still; this was a woman whose daily walks were fuelled by the unpredictability of the march of history, while also always committed to the movement.

The year 1905 was a significant and revolutionary one for Rosa's 'Polish economy' outside of the limelight. It would see the end of her relationship with Leo Jogiches, a break that was inseparable from the radical change in her international stature. She had met him as a relatively unknown PhD student; she left him as a famous and infamous leader of the international Left. In an early letter from 24 April 1900 Rosa raised her concerns with Leo that 'you had stopped loving me; perhaps there is even someone else who has a claim on you, that I at any rate have ceased to be for you the person who would be capable of making you happy in this life – to the extent that it is at all possible.'[46]

Another letter contains some honest reflections on the changes Rosa was experiencing and the new pressures upon her:

> you should remember how often you said to me that for our personal relationship to become normal, you would have to know that I could get along without you! . . . If you only knew how painful it is for me here many times, that I don't consult with anyone, that I don't rely on anyone, and cannot share my doubts with anyone . . . If you wanted to, how wonderfully well we could live together and work together![47]

Clara Zetkin reflected years after that it takes a strong man to bear a strong personality such as Rosa Luxemburg's.[48] Rosa Luxemburg is neither the first woman nor the last to experience a divide between the public and the private. As her comrade and leading light of the Second International Eleanor Marx penned in 1886: 'the life of woman does not coincide with that of man. Their lives do not intersect. In many cases do not even touch. Hence the life of the race is stunted.'[49] Rosa was learning at first hand the realities of the division of the sexes, and she was discovering that no matter how quick her ascent in the international revolutionary world, being a woman would mean living with unique challenges.

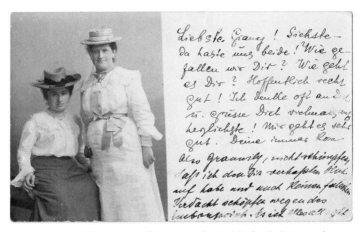

Luise Kautsky and Rosa, next to a letter sent to the Kautsky family (Minna and Luise), 1905.

Whereas publicly Rosa's stature was becoming more established, her relationship with Leo was tested in new ways:

> I need you! We need each other! Truly no other couple has such a mission in this life, as we do, mutually, for each to make a human being out of each other. I feel this with every step I take, and so I feel the pain of our separation more than ever.[50]

Rosa grew busier and busier and the estrangement continued, as she wrote in October 1905: 'Yesterday I received no letter from you, and today you'll receive none from me. But that's not out of revenge. There has been no need of "visits" all day today.'[51] Rosa Luxemburg by this time had a remarkably clear perspective of her life's vocation and the path ahead of her; she was coming to learn the challenges her chosen position would place in front of her that many other women would never have to face:

someday I could certainly enjoy to the fullest the experience of how a person lives who has no (writer's) obligations on their conscience and deals with everything right on time. But I definitely will die without ever having that experience, as the well-known woman in Dickens who died without seeing the end of her tasks. Maybe it would have an effect on me if you [were here and we] were working regularly. What do you think?[52]

Finding a way to balance engagements with her lover and close friends, living a full revolutionary life and ceaselessly writing was becoming trickier for Rosa. Yet her warmth and generosity of spirit shine in examples such as a report by her niece Annie, who had gifted her aunt Rosa an enchanting blue blouse, and received the response, 'I'm terribly happy about it.'[53] Rosa's internal psyche and her wishes for 'a normal life' were as much hindered by her commitment to the revolutionary cause as they had been turbulent during her relationship with Leo.

Sex and power are a dangerous mix, and yet can never be separated. Rosa learnt this through her relationship with Leo. The rest of her love affairs would never reach such emotional heights: her first big love would forever be Leo, alongside whom she entered the world stage. The stress on the relationship became more and more felt, until the decisive break-up. The tone of their letters changed from the early stage of their romance; lust and craving were replaced with matter-of-fact planning and revolutionary updates. Rosa's passionate love affair was interweaved with her political alliance and the dynamic changes taking place in all other levels of her life. And 33-year-old Rosa was not the same woman who fell in love with a passionate revolutionary at eighteen.

Rosa Luxemburg was released from prison on 25 October 1904, suddenly and unexpectedly a month ahead of planned, as she recounted in a letter to her friend Henriette Roland Holst.[54]

The early twentieth century, following her imprisonment, was a period of continual travel for Rosa. Between speaking tours in Germany and her attendance at the Internationals she was rarely still. Ill health haunted her all her life: anaemia, a sensitive stomach, often exhaustion from work and periods of depression – the robust approach to her vocation is all the more impressive when juxtaposed with her physical frailty. Despite this, 1905 would prove to be a crucial year for a woman whose life was underpinned by the concept of revolution. The seeds of dismantling the old regime were being firmly sown in the Russian empire, and Rosa was able to observe her ideas being tested on the ground. 'I do see the strengthening of international feeling to be, in and of itself, a means of fighting against bigotry and ignorance, on which such a goodly part of opportunism rests.'[55]

The revolutionary activity was accelerating history's progression. The 'Revolution of 1905' – a shorthand for events that took place between the end of 1904 and the summer of 1907 – began with a great strike in St Petersburg, the consequences of which shocked the Russian people greatly. It involved 150,000 workers on strike across 382 factories and a period of labour unrest that led to the march of workers to the Winter Palace. On 22 January 1905, known as 'Bloody Sunday', the strikers were on their way to protest the tsar when they were targeted with harsh violence and gunfire, Russian soldiers consequently murdered several hundred factory workers.[56] Rosa's work on this revolution showed her theoretical focus: she only engaged in writing when it achieved practical significance within the march of history.[57] At the same time Rosa was completely emotionally committed to the concept of revolution and living within it, never shying away from turmoil and rupture whatever their cost, as she herself said, 'I live happily in the storm.'[58]

The 1905 revolution was also a catalyst for change in the Polish ranks. The SDKPiL grew from 25,000 to 40,000 members, issuing papers in Polish, Yiddish and German.[59] At the same time, the period didn't distance her – she became more distant during this period. The Polish national question was challenged anew, with some in the PPS-Left (her partisan nemesis from her homeland) swaying towards her position of opposing national self-determination within Poland, yet the party did not merge with the SDKPiL and ideological differences remained.[60] The PPS was better organized than the SDKPiL and they had remained at odds.[61] Rosa revisited the national question within the Polish context and asserted: 'In other words, when revolution broke out, the *only thing* that remained of nationalism was *reaction*, while its *outwardly* and *formally* revolutionary side, that which flaunted the slogan of armed insurrection for national independence, vanished at the first wave of the present revolutionary upsurge, never to be seen again.'[62] The primary role of the proletariat led her to refuse alliances with the peasants and nationalists as much as with the bourgeois liberals. Lenin took this position to a different conclusion; he too refused alliances with liberals who agitated for bourgeois democracy, and yet advocated alliances that strategically allowed him to move his revolutionary cause forward.[63]

These ideological differences heightened ongoing processes of allegiances, loyalties and divergence. One such process was the development of the Bund. The Bund, a group which aimed to unite Jewish workers on the basis on their Jewishness, split from the RSDLP in 1903 due to demands for cultural autonomy. Rosa and Leo both had consistently refused to join the Bund and support its causes. In 1904, before the Amsterdam congress, Rosa sent a letter to Alexander N. Potresov in which she claimed that the Bund was causing divisions under the guise of federalism. At the same time, the Bund preferred Luxemburg and Jogiches to other Polish Marxists, and Luxemburg had published several of her articles in the Bundist paper *Der Yiddischer Arbeter* in 1899. As one of Rosa's biographers, J. P. Nettl, notes, although John Mill, one of the Bund's founders, viewed Luxemburg and Jogiches as resistant to his early appeals, and firmly opposed to any obligation to a specifically Jewish socialist movement, he saw them with an eye that was politically and personally neutral if not overly friendly.[64]

Rosa was never estranged from her own Jewishness, but her relationship to her Jewish roots was – much in line with her entire personality – *sui generis*. In a letter later in life she wrote:

> what do you want with this theme of the 'special suffering of the Jews'? I am just as much concerned with the poor victims on the rubber plantations of Putumayo, the Blacks in Africa with whose corpses the Europeans play catch . . . I have no special place in my heart for the [Jewish] ghetto. I feel at home in the entire world wherever there are clouds and birds and human tears.[65]

Rosa's own Jewishness always gave her the outsider's point of view, yet she shied away from leaning on these perspectives to create cultural or religious loyalties. She did not see the need to organize with her fellow Jews, and certainly not to seek cultural autonomy as a Jewess. Rosa Luxemburg could never be solely defined as a Jew; the human race was her category of reference and the revolution her category of action.

Luxemburg's writing on the Russian Revolution, published as daily reports in the German press, showed the consolidation of her thought and style. She wrote as a form of agitation, and her internationalism not only lies as a theoretical foundation, but was interleaved in the practice of writing itself. Her reports reveal her excitement about the unfolding of the revolution, including specific events and issues. Like many revolutions, that of 1905 was crucial for women. Rosa's approach to the woman question arose out of her commitment to revolutionary socialism, and yet her analysis shows precision and commitment to change in woman's position in society. She wrote forcefully, in an essay titled 'Russian

Rosa, *c.* 1910. 'I feel at home in the entire world wherever there are clouds and birds and human tears.'

Women Workers in the Battle': 'Whoever needs convincing that women are just as capable as men of experiencing both citizenship in its highest sense and the noblest of civic virtues would do well to study the history of the liberation struggles that have shaken Russia since the abolition of serfdom.'[66]

Luxemburg also showed a significant amount of empathy towards the victims of the escalating violence (a very different image to the 'bloody Rosa' stereotype that would haunt her). Specifically, she wrote about the growing anti-Semitic violence unfolding during the revolution. Other themes recur in her accounts: the focus on the eight-hour day ties events in Russia to the overarching agenda of the Second International, exemplifying Rosa's commitment to internationalism in theory and action. The emphasis on the need to free prisoners of conscience and allow freedom of thought in the revolutionary process itself returns in many of her writings. For Rosa, freedom was essential to the revolutionary process itself; emancipation would not start in post-revolutionary society, but rather is part and parcel of the process of liberation.

Rosa's reporting quotes Marx throughout, showing a continuity between his writing (including on bourgeois revolutions) and these events. The emphasis on the need for the working class to emancipate itself occurs throughout the reports. Her loyalty to Poland in these revolutionary times appears, too:

> Social Democracy in our country, just as in Russia – as is usual for all true revolutionary mass movements – could barely keep up with, and give expression to, the feelings and desires of the masses, which had erupted volcanically.[67]

In a letter to Leo Jogiches in 1905, she wrote, 'I'm terribly happy about what our people are doing at home.'[68] The woman of three homelands finally saw them united through revolution. And in a statement that carries great weight, she penned: 'In Russia, as everywhere else in the world, the cause of freedom and of social progress now lies with the class-conscious proletariat. And it is in good hands!'[69]

Daily reporting from afar allowed Luxemburg to develop her analytical focus on the revolutionary events: she wrote on strikes and actions of the working class as emblematic of revolutionary action; the necessity of internationalism and resistance to war; seeing failures and successes as inevitable outcomes of the dialectic between human agency and history; and the intertwining of liberation within the revolutionary cause as a whole. Energetically looking towards the future, she wrote:

> The year 1906 will not be short of storms and battles demanding utter devotion and taking heavy casualties. We can only rely on our hopes that German Social Democracy will know how to fulfill her world-historical-duty as the spearhead of these conflicts, and so I say – *to work, onward to new battles!*[70]

On the morning of 28 December 1905 Rosa Luxemburg, disguised under the pseudonym Anna Matschke, crossed the border into Russia to observe the last stages of the revolution and report on it from the ground.[71] The Kautskys and a few others saw her off from the Friedrichstrasse station in Berlin.[72] A strike on the railway demanded a detour via East Prussia, where her first Prussian experience was a good meal of schnitzel; she then proceeded on another train, the only woman and only civilian on board.[73] Rosa's arrival in Russia for her first revolution was as anti-climactic as her journey.

She had missed the height of the revolution, which proved to be unsuccessful yet vital. In 'The Problem of the "Hundred Peoples"', Rosa referred to the current revolutionary rising of the proletariat as 'the first act in the process of fraternization among the people of tsarist empire', yet the revolution of 1905 was more of a dress rehearsal than a first act.[74] Like all dress rehearsals the intensity felt in this stage of history was high, and she was getting ready for the curtains to rise on the main stage. In another essay, 'In the Bonfire Glow of the Revolution', she claimed that the most important motto is 'to be prepared is everything!'[75] Rosa Luxemburg was preparing herself to march into the next chapter of history, which was to unravel in 1906.

3

The Last Two Men of German Social Democracy

Luxemburg recalled how one time she and Clara Zetkin, her comrade since arriving in Berlin at the turn of the century, were running late for a dinner at the house of the founder of the SPD, August Bebel, after getting carried away on their shared walk. En route, they composed their epitaph: 'here lie the last two men of German social democracy.'

Rosa Luxemburg, half of the 'last two men' of German social democracy, was again incarcerated for her revolutionary work in Warsaw at the end of the Russian Revolution in 1906, for her involvement in revolutionary activities, and then bailed out of prison by her brother Jozef for 3,000 rubles.[1] Rosa's health was ailing and she was weak due to the distress of her shared cell, hunger strikes and other pressures of confinement. In August 1906 Rosa went to Kuokkala, Finland, to recuperate from her imprisonment and reside with the movers and shakers of the 1905 revolution, Lenin and Trotksy. Her presence of mind rapidly recovered there, as did her physical health. She had been unable to write in her shared prison cell, and with the new-found freedom to discuss and reflect came the ability to express in words on her experiences and the lessons learned of the 1905 revolution. Rosa's sharp tongue was quickly restored, as she wrote to the Kautskys: 'by God, the revolution is great and strong as long as the Social Democrats don't smash it up.'[2]

The 1905 revolution was pivotal for Rosa Luxemburg. She wrote a text at the request of the Hamburg Provincial Party that, together

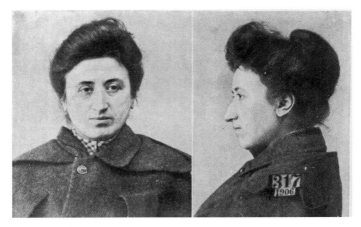

Rosa's mugshot, 1906, Warsaw, shortly after the revolution of 1905. She was imprisoned first in 1904 and from then on was intermittently incarcerated for dissenting against official policies, in many cases supported by her own party, the SPD.

with her reporting from the revolution itself, was crucial for inscribing through her unique prism the lessons she had learned from 1905 and its place within world history. *The Mass Strike, Political Party and Trade Unions* aimed to interpret the events of 1905–6 and the future of class struggle in Germany for German workers.[3] German trade-union membership numbered around 1,500,000 people: about one-tenth of the working class.[4] Rosa's impressions of the power of the mass strike in Russia stood in stark contrast to the policy advocated by the SPD and trade union leaders that opposed the strike as a tactic. At the party congress at Jena, a weak resolution that failed to throw weight behind the mass strike as a legitimate device was followed by an SPD party congress in which even a theoretical discussion of the mass strike was banned. The Jena resolution, which argued that the turn to mass strike would only occur on the condition that the government refused to adhere to demands for suffrage, was reversed by the end of 1906. This buried the Jena resolution finally, and was political grounds for Rosa Luxemburg to turn to the mass strike as a central concept in her revolutionary theory. In her use of the term 'labour of Sisyphus' in *Reform or Revolution* (1900) she had stirred the indignation of trade union leaders. Yet when Karl Kautsky in 1908 published his *Road to Power* he used the concept in the same way, but it was received by exactly the same people with great delight, showing just how much reception of these authors' work depends on the perception of their personality, not on their argument.

Rosa Luxemburg identified the crucial role of the mass strike in the 1905 revolution. Her main argument was that the mass strike was not an artificial product imposed from above; it was the way the proletariat could forge its consciousness, in the words of Mary-Alice Waters when introducing the text, 'not a crafty method discovered by subtle reasoning for the purpose of making the proletarian struggle more effective, but *the method of motion of the proletarian mass*, the phenomenal form of the proletarian struggle in the revolution'.[5] Rosa's statement was not only an ideological but a political intervention against the German trade union leaders who she came to see as her most serious opponents. Luxemburg shows a theoretical contradiction in the trade unions' disagreement in supporting mass strikes: either workers are not in a stage of history (in terms of preparation and resources) in which they are prepared for the mass strike, or they don't need to strike. Luxemburg thus places the argument between the anarchist theory of the mass strike – for its own sake – and the conservative interpretation of strikes that preceded 1905. Luxemburg's commitment to both theory and practice is elucidated in a clear form here: the strike is essential to the revolution as it is part of historical dialectics; it is not outside of the process, a goal in and of itself, as would argue anarchists, but rather integral to the social democratic process. *The Mass Strike, Political Party and Trade Unions* discusses the politics around the Jena congress and the moves of each of the parties that led her to her theoretical conclusion.

Luxemburg discusses different types of strikes – specifically, the distinction between economic and political strikes – as well as the struggle for the eight-hour day, which stood at the epicentre of the agenda of the Second International, and focuses on some of the practical aspects of strikes: their continuity, the combination of political and economic factors and strata, and their inseparability from the revolutionary struggle: 'Every great mass strike repeats, on a smaller scale, the entire history of the Russian mass strike. The economic struggle is the transmitter from one political center to another; the political struggle is the periodic fertilization of the soil for the economic struggle.'[6] Events in Russia showed her that the mass strike was inseparable from the revolution. At her argument's crescendo, she said:

> the mass strike is the first natural, impulsive form of every great revolutionary struggle of the proletariat and the more highly developed antagonism is between capital and labour, the more effective and decisive must mass strike become.[7]

Luxemburg's text highlights not only her deep understanding of the role revolutionary processes play within the development of the consciousness of the working classes, but the centrality of the mass strike within this conception of socialism from the ground up: from the masses.

Rosa and her comrades agreed that the Russian Revolution was a bourgeois liberal revolution. Lenin gave a lecture on the 1905 revolution in which he argued, much like Luxemburg, for an emphasis on a combination of economic and political strikes at the epicentre of the mass strike.[8] Lenin argued against the idea that workers overestimated their strength; he proposed that the gains of revolution could only be seen when they benefited not only the working class but the whole of society. Moreover, Lenin understood that the break-up of state order was caused by the intertwining of political demands and economic demands, which were solely in the interest of the working class. For Rosa, by contrast, the mass strike and the revolution to which it is central always occur as revolutionary actions by the working class.

The Mass Strike, Political Party and Trade Unions exemplifies Luxemburg's internationalism, her intermeshing of theory and historical discussion, her commitment to Marxian dialectics in the contemporary struggle and above all her lifelong commitment to revolution as practice. Ever since her first full-length work based on her PhD thesis, all of Luxemburg's sources, as well as her conclusions to the works she had authored, assumed that action taking place beyond one country was essential for revolutionary action. Her development as a thinker and agitator allowed her to consolidate and expand this belief. The Marxist Karl Radek stated in 1921 that Luxemburg's essay on the Russian Revolution of 1905 was the first document of German communism.[9] The uniqueness of the Russian Revolution was that the overthrow of an absolutist state occurred simultaneously with the invigoration of the power of the working class.

The emphasis on democracy and political education in action led to a new venture to add to Rosa's already long list of qualifications. When it was suggested to Rosa that she take a position in the newly established Trade Union School in Berlin, she was not thrilled at first. 'My interest in the school as a whole is lukewarm, and I was not born to be a schoolteacher.'[10] She was compelled to accept the offer, however, due to the prospect of a regular income. This position proved crucial for Rosa's intellectual development as well as her social and political life. She taught between 1907 (a year after the school's founding) and 1914, and was the only woman on the teaching staff. Her workload was heavy; she taught for five days a week for two hours a day, and helped students at the school beyond that.[11] Moreover, Rosa discovered that teaching helped elucidate ideas in her mind. She also taught history, economics and social theory at the German SPD school, a school for working-class people that was part of the growing influence of the SPD. Her explanations of complex economic and political theories, and other intricate issues, were punctuated with literary and cultural references, from Shakespeare and Dostoevsky to physics, showing her intellectual creativity. Her work in the school was crystallized within the context of her life's work: 'What the masses lack is general enlightenment, the theory which gives us the possibility of systematizing the hard facts and forging them into a deadly weapon to use against our opponents.'[12] Rosa reflected on her philosophy of teaching:

> We have tried to make clear to them . . . that they must continue to go on learning, that they will go on learning all their lives . . . what the masses need is general education, theory which gives them the chance of making a system out of the detail acquired from experience and which helps them to forge a weapon against our enemies.[13]

Her student Rosi Wolfstein once recalled:

> How did she bring us to critically reflect and independently interrogate questions of social democracy? By means of questions! She tapped along the walls of our knowledge and thus enabled us to hear for ourselves where and how it sounded hollow. She explored arguments and made us see for ourselves if they were sound, and by encouraging us to acknowledge our errors, she led us to develop an airtight solution.[14]

Crucially Wolfstein remembered Rosa's analytical clarity in 'isolating the essentials' rather than relying on rhetoric 'which rendered her such a magnificent speaker and made one tremble in awe of this woman's universal intellect'.[15] On the basis of her

Rosa Luxemburg in the Trade Union School, 1911, seen in the back. A beloved and sharp-minded teacher, the period of her teaching was one of the most productive in her professional life.

lectures and discussions at school she decided to work on a full-length book, eventually called *Introduction to Political Economy*. She began conducting research for the book at the end of 1907 and by summer 1908 was already preparing a manuscript for the printer.[16]

In a letter to Clara Zetkin, Rosa mused that *Introduction to Political Economy* 'is not an economic history, as you thought, but a brief analysis of political economy, that is, of capitalist mode of production'.[17] This text, as well as others written by Luxemburg while she worked as a teacher, shows us her breadth and depth of knowledge and analytical clarity. It is highly illustrative of her independence of mind in working within the Marxist tradition while asserting her own unique voice. Rather than abstracting, she presents a rigorous historical approach by discussing the factors that helped bring the capitalist production process through its commodity forms and production of values into being. However, her aim was not so much to write a history of capitalism as to discuss the central categories of Marx's idea of capital through a historical approach. Rosa the teacher brought her brilliance and originality into the classroom. Elsewhere she wrote,

> I feel, in a word, the need as [Wladyslaw] Heine would say, to 'say something great' . . . I feel that within me there is maturing a completely new and original form which dispenses with the usual formulas and patterns and breaks them down . . . I feel the utter certainty that something is there, that something will be born.[18]

Rosa Luxemburg had consistently refused to be defined in the terms of her contemporaries or to accept restrictions within Marxian thinking. Her thinking was original in both form and content. The argument of the text proceeds clearly throughout, allowing her students to walk with her through the underpinning question: what is political economy? What does that conceptual field mean in and of itself? Rosa's text starts by asserting that political economy is 'a curious science' and it is hard to demarcate 'the object of this science'.[19] She then shows the narrowness of perception as well as the conceptual confusion in 'specialists' discussions' of the idea of national economy. She shows, throughout, that 'national economy' is used interchangeably with political economy, without explaining the meaning of either: 'It is precisely – the theory of national economy. What are horn-rimmed spectacles? Spectacles with a horn rim.'[20] Her sharp analysis, irreverence to any kind of authority and witty sense of humour allow us to think of Rosa's class of students as a group that could perhaps disagree with her, but always follow her without ever becoming bored.

Luxemburg discusses a conceptual bias that shows the analytical framework she critiques as flawed and tautological. Rosa honed the focus on understanding the crisis within capitalism that forces it to expand internationally; at the same time, capitalism created new crises and opportunities for disillusion. Capitalism is a historical phenomenon but not a necessary one for perpetuity. Rosa created an agency within the reader that would allow them to understand how they are able to intervene in and work to dismantle capitalism.

> If it is the task and object of political economy to explain the laws of the origin, development and spread of the capitalist mode of production, it is an unavoidable consequence that it must as a further consequence also discover the laws of the decline of capitalism, which just like previous economic forms is not of eternal duration, but is simply a transitional phase of history, a rung on the endless ladder of social development. The doctrine of the emergence of capital thus logically turns into the doctrine of the decline of capitalism.[21]

She continued: 'great creators of political economy lived in the rock-solid conviction that the present capitalist social-order, in which everything is a commodity and produced only for trade, is the only possible and eternal social order, which will endure as long as there are people on this earth.'[22] The main focus for Luxemburg was dismantling capitalism through the act of writing itself.

A crucial contribution from this text is Luxemburg's unwavering commitment to dismiss the idea of national economy in any form. Luxemburg crafted into her argument proof that, for bourgeois economists, the non-Marxist reading of political economy also assumes there is such a thing as national economy, an economy that can be contained within a nation-state. This is an idea she refuses point blank: 'one thing, at any rate, is established: in all definitions of bourgeois specialists we have cited above, it is always a question of "national economy".'[23] Rosa Luxemburg sharply disagreed with that position.

Luxemburg instead proceeded to show interdependences among world economies of commodities, labour and production.[24] She argued clearly:

in light of such a tremendously developed reciprocal
exchange, how are we to draw the borders between the
'economy' of one nation and that of another? Should we
speak of so many 'national economies' as if these could
be treated as separate territories in economic terms?[25]

For there could never be socialism contained in one country,
since no political economy can exist in isolation. Moreover, this
conceptual problem carries political weight. The discussion moves
very swiftly into showing how the use of the term 'national' is most
often used in conjunction with imperialism and colonialism. Rosa,
however, moved the argument on:

within each European industrial country, capitalist production
ceaselessly drives out petty trade, handicraft and small
peasant production. At the same time it draws all backward
European countries, and all the lands of America, Asia,
Africa and Australia, into the world economy. This happens
in two ways: by world trade and by colonial conquests.[26]

Patriarchal capitalism is anarchic and international; so must its
critique be in order to challenge it from its core. There is no use
in writing on the concept of 'national economy'; thus we cannot
assume that political economy, which is conflated in the theory of
her time to national economy, holds any analytical and conceptual
power.

Introduction to Political Economy is a grossly under-read and
under-examined text. It has, however, two crucial flaws within its
argument. First, a logical tautology regarding the creation of private
property mars the discussion. It is unclear in Rosa's historical
proceeding what happens first; does private property emerge as a
result of generalized commodity exchange, or is it the other way
around? Second, a flaw that will run through her entire work,

Luxemburg presents an irresolvable tension between capitalism as anarchy and socialism as state organization.

Rosa's teaching at the Trade Union School introduced to her one of her most significant companions, whose four-pawed amble would accompany Rosa's march to come, in all its ups and downs. Mimi, a little, injured kitten found after class one day, was named by Rosa no doubt after the heroine of Puccini's *La Bohème*, a work inscribed within opera-loving Rosa's psyche. Rosa's relationship with Mimi is telling of her contradictions. She had loved animals since childhood, but the few other pets in the Luxemburg household did not achieve the longevity and centrality of Mimi's reign. Rosa had once kept in her flat a rabbit, which troubled her neighbours, who were less enthused about the new inhabitant. She used to feed pricey white bread to a goat she saw every time she visited the dentist.[27] Yet Mimi occupied a different position. Mimi became, quickly, a central feature of Rosa's 'Polish economy'. Rosa's friend Mathilde Jacob recalled an invitation from Rosa: 'you must visit me sometime: first of all because of Mimi, second to see my paintings and third to give me pleasure.'[28] Mimi was a consistent interlocutor for Rosa from this point onwards; she never wavered in her love and devotion for her feline friend.

The years that followed 1906 brought many revolutions and upheavals into Rosa's life. After her first great love and comrade Leo Jogiches, another man entered Rosa's life. Konstantin 'Kostja' Zetkin, who was fourteen years her junior and son of her closest woman friend and comrade Clara Zetkin, became her lover and confidante. From its start, the relationship followed a different dynamic to that with Leo. The 35-year-old Rosa was assured, confident and internationally recognized. Kostja was mentored by her, guided by her as an economist and a thinker, and brought into the staff of the Trade Union School at her recommendation. Her relationships post-Leo caused her first lover's violent temper to explode.

Rosa Luxemburg walking, holding her beloved cat Mimi (alongside fellow socialist Antonin Nemec).

L[eo] won't let me go and declares that he would sooner kill me. [He says] I'll be staying here even in a hospital . . . we went directly [from the bus] into an elegant restaurant, where my brother was expecting me for dinner. A fine orchestra was playing, in the gallery, music from the last scene of Carmen, and while they were playing L[eo] softly whispered to me: 'I would sooner strike you dead.'[29]

Despite no longer living together (which was Leo's choice), Leo retained a key to Rosa's apartment and refused to return it. As a result, Rosa bought a gun as a means of self-protection.[30] In the opera, the eponymous Carmen pleads of Don José, 'kill me at once, or let me go,' but Rosa is no Carmen, and she knew at first hand that her freedom was her most precious commodity. Psychological, emotional and physical abuse had left their marks: 'I can't get away from him here, but also everything in me rebels against sneaking away like some sort of slave.'[31] Rosa's life was always motivated by freedom articulated through action and yet deep trauma and bruises in a woman's psyche cannot be easily erased. Leo enacted violence on her repeatedly, controlling her environment and intimidating her, taking the keys to her home from her maid and stalking her. For an independent mind and an intense spirit willing to throw herself into the revolution head first, intimate violence provided a very different darkness.

Nevertheless, the relationship with Kostja continued, despite threats from Leo and the need to hide it from many with whom Kostja and Rosa collaborated. Kostja sent her flowers; she reported back on operas. Mimi the cat functioned in the letters as the child Rosa never had. Rosa often signed her letters 'R and M', and reported feline behaviours and funny quirks. 'Mimi is a scoundrel. She leaped at me from the floor and tried to bite me. I kiss you. Mimi does too.'[32] Rosa expressed her yearning to go on hikes in Switzerland with Kostja, gave him writing advice and commented on various circles they both moved within. However, the letter exchange lacks the sexual and emotional intensity her exchanges with Leo contained. She has many emotional registers, and yet vibrancy and wit accompany her pen: 'Darling, do avoid risks! Just think [how you would feel] if you knew I was constantly hovering over abysses.'[33] Rosa herself never moved far from the abyss, in any sphere of her life. But her resilience was unique: 'I am going to work with pleasure and love and am determined to bring more strictness, clarity, and chasteness into my life. This conception of life for me has grown to maturity in dealing with you and therefore it is fitting for you to hear those words.'[34] 'L'amour est un oiseau rebelle,' sings Carmen; love is a rebellious bird. Love, sex and happiness are never unequivocal, never controllable; not even for Rosa Luxemburg, the greatest mind since Marx.

Rosa's multifaceted psyche and lifelong passion for the arts found new outlets when she embraced a self-education in drawing and painting. In this period her engagement with the arts became more and more serious and she proudly shared some of her sketches and drawings with her friends and interlocutors. She drew many sketches of Kostja and attempted to paint landscapes as well as a few self-portraits and images of workers on trains. There was no area of life that would be simply a hobby for Rosa; she threw herself with the same passion and devotion into drawing as she did with all other spheres of interest.

London in the spring has its own special charms, though Rosa was, so it seems, not particularly susceptible to them. She travelled to the city in early 1907 for the Fifth Congress of the Russian Social Democratic Labour Party, to discuss with the great movers and shakers of the Russian Revolution of 1905 its consequences as well as the proposed strategy for what was to come next. Rosa stayed in a beautiful Victorian house at 66 Goldhurst Terrace, but she complained about the noise and the distractions of city life. Yet, the rain and gloom

Rosa Luxemburg and Konstantin (Kostja) Zetkin holding a painting of Zetkin by Luxemburg, 1907. Rosa was a talented self-trained artist, and shared her art with her close friends and comrades.

as well as the budding of spring made it an appropriate setting to discuss the revolution that had been nipped in its bud.[35]

Discussion of the tasks of the proletariat in the bourgeois-democratic revolution made the split between the Mensheviks and the Bolsheviks all too clear. The main disputed issues were whether to start an armed uprising against the tsar and how to handle trade unions. Mensheviks argued for incremental change through a workers' congress that would transform the Russian Social Democratic Labour Party into a Westernized social democratic party. Bolsheviks held the more revolutionary lines, which were elucidated in a speech by Lenin, quoted and inscribed by another comrade. Rosa was once again noted to be on the revolutionary side:

'Our old disputes, our theoretical, and especially our tactical, differences are constantly being converted, in the course of the revolution, into the most downright practical differences.' A young delegate, Joseph Stalin, reported: 'Of exceptional interest were the speeches of Comrade Rosa Luxemburg, who conveyed greetings to the congress on behalf of the German Social-Democrats and expounded the views of our German comrades on our disagreements.'[36]

Rosa took the Bolshevik side in this debate, but the differences between Luxemburg and that faction had become apparent since the discussion of the strike.

Rosa and Lenin had a warm relationship, turbulent at times, revealed in this letter to Kostja Zetkin of 1911:

Mimi keeps going Kuru! She impressed Lenin tremendously, he said that only in Siberia had he seen such a magnificent creature, that she was a *barskii kot* – a majestic cat. She also flirted with him, rolled on her back and behaved enticingly toward him, but when he tried to approach her she whacked him with a paw and snarled like a tiger.[37]

Throughout her life Rosa's relationships with her female friends and comrades sustained her emotionally, nourished her politically and inspired her personally. She did not agree with them on all matters, and owing to her bad temper, fights and arguments often broke out, but her kindness and generosity always enabled amends to be made with those that mattered most to her. Clara Zetkin, Luise Kautsky, Sophie Liebknecht and Mathilde Jacob are just several of the women who would accompany Luxemburg through her life and her relationships with them were as fundamental to understanding her psyche as her relationships with lovers and comrades. Jacob was strongly committed to Luxemburg and served

Group photo of the International Socialist Bureau, 1907. Lenin can be seen at the front; Rosa is two people away from him. Despite disagreeing on many ideological positions, Lenin and Rosa had mutual respect and engaged warmly with each other throughout their professional lives.

as her right hand. Much material as well as recollections of Rosa are due to Jacob's work in preserving her friend's legacy, and to her work as typesetter, yet Jacob herself was erased from history. Zetkin, especially, will be remembered as a ground-breaking socialist feminist whose speech in the 1889 Paris International, translated by Eleanor Marx, set the terms for debates around women within socialism. In 1910 Zetkin seconded Luise Zietz's proposal in the Socialist Women Conference for International Women's Day. A photograph from 1910 shows Clara and Rosa walking together, with Rosa wearing an unusually flamboyant checked skirt and an elegant hat. Luise Kautsky, on the other hand, may have revealed the champagne-loving socialist in Rosa: 'That's exactly what I love about you, that I can always put you in a champagne mood, with life making our fingers tingle and us ready for any kind of foolishness.'[38] The intimate Rosa, a faithful and

Rosa Luxemburg walking with Clara Zetkin, 1910, the same year Zetkin and Luise Zietz founded International Women's Day. Rosa worked closely with her women comrades and any debate of her views on women must be read in the context of those collaborations, which always blurred the boundaries between official politics and personal relationships.

loving friend, is revealed in these relationships. Rosa was becoming more aware that within a sexist world in which she was targeted for multiple reasons, her women comrades could be a pillar of strength on the march. She retained connections with her family as much as she could despite living an increasingly turbulent life. In particular, her niece Annie, a talented musician who shared her aunt's love for the arts, became a frequent visitor to Rosa's apartment, often going with her to concerts and the theatre or getting cheap tickets for Rosa to attend events with her comrades.

Rosa Luxemburg's significant place at the time within socialist debates elicited as much venom and hatred as it did camaraderie and discussion. She was never part of the SPD's inner circle, which was essentially older men.[39] The Austrian socialist and labour leader Victor Adler wrote to August Bebel, chairman of the SPD: 'The poisonous bitch will yet do a lot of damage, all the more so because she is as clever as a monkey [*blitzgescheit*] while on the other hand her sense of responsibility is totally lacking and her only motive is an almost pervasive desire for self-justification.'[40] Her combative nature baffled her comrades, as can be seen in trade unionist responses to her intervention in the revisionist debate: 'One should always be polite to ladies, but Comrade Rosa Luxemburg will certainly not insist on velvet gloves in political matters.'[41] Rosa's insistence on ideological integrity was part of her way to fight back against sexism. Even within the German Communist Party she was dubbed 'the syphilis of the Commintern'.[42] Fellow socialist Rosa Levine-Meyer recalls her husband, Eugen Levine, commenting to her on the street: 'there goes a woman of quite extraordinary brain. She *frightens me.*'[43]

Rosa was a disabled woman who walked with a limp throughout her life. Her understanding of gender and the multidimensional nature of oppression – never seen only through one lens of gender, unlike the bourgeois feminists – perhaps links to the fact that she herself knew multiple layers of oppression. Her writing on

Rosa speaking to a crowd at Stuttgart, outside the Congress of the Second International, 1907.

disability only occurs in sporadic places in the archive, and yet she was always attentive towards all those who may have been affected disproportionately by capitalism. At the same time, she always refused to be characterized by a unidimensional identity.

Rosa's Jewishness drew attacks on herself and her surroundings, as she articulated in a letter from 1910:

> the entire bourgeois press has pulled out all the stops against us. In the process – and this is what's most noteworthy – the attacks on us have come from above all the so-called progressive press . . . And the main point is that this 'Free Thought' publication has suddenly begun preaching against us with the slogan 'down with the Jews!' – and the entire liberal, progressive press has abandoned itself to an all-out orgy of anti-semitism. Socialists are 'Jews', our Mtot [hammer] is an organ of 'the Jewish syndicate', we are all agents of 'Jewry', and the progressive press is overflowing with personal slander and vulgarity.[44]

Rosa was targeted by both sexism and anti-Semitism, yet she never desisted from struggling with the sharpest weapon she had: her mind. Her understanding of the complexity of oppression never reduced her ability for action; in fact it guided her activism and thinking. And that complexity underpinned the focus of her work, which was becoming clearer, especially in this period of her life: it never overlooked any strata of oppression.

In 1912 Rosa's organizational home was the SPD and that was the location of her theoretical work and agitation. Rosa weighed in on the issue of women's suffrage. Her argument was sharp, timely and, like the rest of her canon, unequivocally defended universal suffrage:

> The capitalist state has not been able to keep women from taking on all these duties and efforts of political life. Step by step, the state has indeed been forced to grant and guarantee them this possibility by allowing them union and assembly rights. Only the last political right is denied women: the right to vote, to decide directly on the people's representatives in legislature and administration, to be an elected member of these bodies.[45]

Here, she notes that the authorities were trying to stop the transformation from even 'getting started', and yet 'the present state gave in to the women of the proletariat when it admitted them to public assemblies, to political associations. And the state did not grant this voluntarily, but out of necessity, under the irresistible pressure of the rising working class.'[46] It was the proletarian class struggle that swept working women into the whirlpool of political life, she claims.

> Using their right of union and assembly, proletarian women have taken a most active part in parliamentary life and in election campaigns. It is only the inevitable consequence, only the logical result of the movement that today millions of proletarian women call defiantly and with self-confidence: *Let us have suffrage!*[47]

She proceeded to argue that whereas women's suffrage was the goal, the mass movement to achieve it was not a job for women alone, but a concern for the entire working class, the men and women of the proletariat. Always a champion of revolutionary democracy, her focus remained on education; on gaining and expanding political access for women and getting their voices heard, especially proletarian women. Rosa was not a bourgeois feminist, defending suffrage for middle-class women (she noted that the state was acting to withhold the vote from working women alone).[48] But suffrage for her was a part of wider issues, the larger state of oppression that she was fighting. For Rosa, education and involvement in the movement were the means by which this oppression would be overcome – it would take more to induce change than merely casting votes at a ballot. She argued that the female proletariat were the ones pushing for universal suffrage and responsible for intensifying the proletarian class struggle: 'This is why bourgeois society abhors and fears women's suffrage. And this is why we want and will achieve it. Fighting for women's suffrage, we will also hasten the coming of the hour when the present society falls in ruins under the hammer strokes of the revolutionary proletariat.'[49] Like Clara Zetkin and Eleanor Marx, the foremother of socialist feminism, Rosa could never separate the woman question from the class question, and observed the fear of empowered women that was instilled at the heart of patriarchal capitalism through utilizing the power of working women in all spheres of social democracy.

Karl Marx's *Capital: A Critique of Political Economy*, one of his most crucial and foundational works, was published in 1867. In his own words, it aimed to reveal 'the economic law of motion of modern society'.[50] Marx aimed to uncover the general process of historical change, and to extend this understanding both to different phases of history as well as particular types of societies. Human beings exist as products of specific historical contexts; they are labouring, social creatures who find expression in generating value in work and in solidarity with their fellow humans. Marx's focus was on capitalism, the system which was the backdrop to his writing in Victorian England, and, according to his reading, alienates people from their human potential. Marx interpreted capital as a process, value in motion. The definition of capital cannot be divorced from the human choice to use monetary circulation as means of exchange within our economic-social system.[51] The labour theory of value stresses that the relationship between exchange, prices and values reflects different social relations of production, distribution and exchange.[52] The worker sells power to the capitalist, who determines how power should be exercised as labour to produce particular commodities.[53] To distinguish the workers themselves from their ability to work, Marx terms the latter 'Labour power'.[54] Labour power exists as a capacity of the working individual, the human being. In a letter to Engels dated 24 August 1867, Marx wrote: 'the best points in my book are: (1) the double character of labour, according to where it is expressed in use value or exchange value . . . (2) the treatment of surplus value independently of its particular forms as profit, interest, ground rent, etc.'[55]

Marx states that for capitalists, as well as the producers, social relations are constituted as material relations between things as well as social relations between persons. Rather than a misrepresentation of reality that can be corrected on empirical grounds, we are driven towards a crucial question: how can we undo the situation in which social relations are conducted as economic relations? The clash between capitalist and non-capitalist societies is crucial in Marx's work.

In 1912, Luxemburg worked on her most significant and comprehensive response to Marx (specifically the second volume of *Capital*) in her third book, *The Accumulation of Capital* (1913), which followed *The Industrial Development of Poland* and *Social Reform or Revolution*. Her *Accumulation of Capital: An Anti-critique* quickly followed in 1915 as a response to the uproar caused by the original work. She reflected in a letter on the process of writing *The Accumulation of Capital* years later:

> The period whilst I was writing 'the Accumulation' was one of the happiest of my life. I lived almost in an ecstasy, seeing and hearing nothing but the problem I was working on so satisfactorily. I don't know what gave me more pleasure: the intellectual wrestling with a knotty point and its gradual unraveling walking slowly up and down the room, or afterwards the putting of results in literary form. Do you know I wrote the lot right off inside four months? A herculean performance. And then I gave the MS. into print without even looking through it again.[56]

The work was developed from a question that emerged when she was writing *Introduction to Political Economy*, in which she devoted nearly half the text to non-capitalist societies. In 'What Is Political Economy?' Luxemburg reflected on the penetration of the capitalist world into the non-capitalist world. *The Accumulation of Capital* was to tackle this relationship head on.

Luxemburg's central argument is simple yet brilliant. In order to sustain demand outside of capitalist economies – as capitalists cannot merely buy only their own commodities and change their surplus value for more commodities – capitalism seeks expansion into non-capitalist societies which create demand outside of their markets.[57]

As the precondition for, as well as the consequence of, accumulation, capitalist production expands more and more into non-capitalist markets. Rosa's internationalism is apparent in the text, as she analyses a range of case studies from the USA to China, South Africa and Canada.

Following Marx, Luxemburg focused her analysis on crises in order to dismantle capitalism through her writing, and carried forward the interpretation of capital and its expansion as a process.

Capitalist reproduction presents a most distinct figure.
In all other economic forms, reproduction proceeds as a
regular and uninterrupted cycle, except in cases of external,
violent interference. Capitalist reproduction, however, to
use a well-known expression of Sismondi's, can only be
presented as a continuous sequence of individual spirals
coiling upwards in an increasing radius from a narrow base
and eventually becoming extremely large. This is followed
by a contraction, and a new spiral starts again with small
loops, tracing the same figure until the next interruption.[58]

She proceeded to argue that 'If capitalist production can act
without restriction as its own consumer, i.e. if production and
market are identical, it becomes totally impossible to explain
the periodic occurrence of crises.'[59] Marx took ideas from
Malthus (without referencing him), claiming that there was a
tendency towards deficiency of demand in the market for surplus
commodities that capitalists produce to create surplus value.
The question arises: who has purchasing power to buy those
commodities? This creates a structural explanation for a non-
productive consuming class.[60] Luxemburg expands this argument
from Malthus via Marx and develops it into an economic
explanation for imperialism, which creates non-capitalist markets
for capitalist commodities. The motivation for Luxemburg's
theoretical analysis is this conundrum in Marx via Malthus, as
well as, crucially, the politically motivated burning question of
imperialism, central to her time:

as much as imperialism is a historical method to prolong
the existence of capital, objectively it is at the same time the
surest way to bring this existence to the swiftest conclusion.
This does not mean that this endpoint has literally to be
reached. The tendency toward this terminal point of capitalist

Rosa at her desk, in her house in Berlin, 1907.

development manifests itself in forms that configure the final phase of capitalism as a period of catastrophes.[61]

She concludes by arguing that capitalism is an economy that must extend itself outside of its own remits; thus it necessitates political mechanisms that ensure its expansion:

> Capitalism is the first form of economy with propagandistic power; it is a form that tends to extend itself over the globe and eradicate all other forms of economy – it tolerates no other alongside itself . . . In itself, it is a living, historical contradiction; the moment of its accumulation is the expression, the continual solution, and simultaneously the exacerbation of this contradiction. At a certain level of its development, this contradiction cannot be solved by any means other than the application of the fundaments of socialism – i.e. the very form of economy that is inherently a universal one and simultaneously a harmonious system in itself, since it is orientated not to accumulation, but to the satisfaction of the vital needs of laboring humanity itself through the development of all of the world's productive powers.[62]

Capitalism can only be overturned by socialism, as it will incrementally expand into any other non-capitalist economy.

Luxemburg's work was a conceptual, theoretical, methodological and historical response to Marx's canon. The work was met with a cacophony of dissent and resentment, which elicited her to write her 'anti-critique'. Luxemburg nonetheless understood that dissent against her ideas was a facet of Marxist tradition, which sees theory advancing through contradiction: 'Sorrowful souls will once again bemoan that "the Marxists are fighting among themselves" . . . But Marxism does not consist of a dozen persons who have granted each other the right to be "experts", before whom the masses are spouses to prostate themselves in blind obedience.'[63] The themes of *Accumulation of Capital* were a lifelong engagement for her, but this text is the clearest articulation of her arguments and intervention in the Marxist canon.

This text also signifies Rosa's overarching response to the centrality of imperialism in the public debate of her time, and her staunch internationalism. In it, Rosa drew on a range of examples from around the world, for example, the South African War, a series of armed conflicts between the British and non-British settlers of South Africa. The 'Boers' – Afrikaans for farmers – refused to grant political rights to non-Boers, both African and British. The British, engaging in a more modern form of warfare, utilized new kinds of weapons, and employed concentration camps for civilians. It was the Africans who paid the highest price for these wars. Rosa analysed the connection between the war and the military organization of the British army. In *Accumulation of Capital* Rosa noted that 'just as the American farmer drove the American Indians westward under pressure from capitalist economy, so the Boers drove Black Africans northward.'[64] The argument continues: 'It was not only the Blacks of the Boer republics who emerged empty-handed from this process; those of the Cape Colony, whom the British government had previously granted equal rights, also found these partially withdrawn from them.'[65] Luxemburg's analysis of imperialism and colonialism as well as her focus on those who would pay the heftiest price for their impact – her anti-imperialism and attentiveness to the oppressed – lie at the heart of her work which sought to offer a solution to a central problem in Marx's writing.

The immediate reception of the *Accumulation of Capital* was overwhelmingly negative (with the exceptions of Franz Mehring and Rosa's old Polish comrade Julian Marchlewski). The right-wing members of the SPD (which at times supported colonial intervention and imperialism more broadly) rejected Luxemburg's thesis. For them, imperialism could be modified to be part and parcel of their outlook on socialism.[66] Gustav Eckstein, an important member at the centre of the SPD, attacked both the theoretical and political angles of her argument. Both those critiques did not see crisis as central to historical development within Luxemburg's theory of the role of imperialism within capitalism.[67] On the Left Rosa did not win many friends either; Antonie Pannekoek, a Dutch Marxist and astronomer, wrote a detailed critique of the work, tackling some of her theoretical assumptions as well as her historical placement of modern colonialism within that of the seventeenth and eighteenth centuries. Pannekoek's criticism was approved by Lenin, who wrote after the publication of *Accumulation of Capital*: 'I have read Rosa's new book *Die Akkumulation des Kapitals*. She has got into a shocking muddle. She has distorted Marx. I am very glad that Pannekoek and Eckstein and Otto Bauer have all with one accord condemned her, and said against her what I said in 1899 against the Narodniks.'[68] In the handwritten marginal notes to his *Accumulation of Capital*, Lenin wrote: 'the description of the torture of Negroes in South America is noisy, colorful and meaningless. Above all it is "non-Marxist".'[69] Lenin was reading the work in 1913, at the lowest point in his relationship with Rosa.

The publication of *Accumulation of Capital* would position Rosa Luxemburg as a significant thinker in the Marxist tradition, as not only a Last Man of German Social Democracy, but a giant woman of Marxism. In 1913, in a new essay on the mass strike, she wrote: 'History will do its work. See that you too do your work.'[70] Rosa's life was a flurry of activity. She certainly was doing her work, and history was about to do its work in unexpected ways. Running late to the house of Bebel while on a walk with Clara would be the least of the challenges Rosa would face within the SPD, as a moment of crisis in her march alongside history was fast approaching.

4

The Countess of Wronke Fortress

For Easter 1908 Rosa went with Karl and Luise Kautsky on a working holiday. Rosa reported:

> Outwardly of course one sees nothing at all of this from me, I go for walks with K, lie in the sun, etc. but I have such uneasiness within me that I would like best to go traveling again immediately or at least go hiking a lot, to climb, to go on camping trips. Unfortunately K doesn't want to do any of those things, doesn't want to climb or hike anywhere, doesn't want to see things, just wants to sit around on the balcony or on the grass.[1]

Disappointed with Kautsky and finding him 'heavy, dull, unimaginative', Rosa failed to persuade him to join her in her daily routine of hard concentrated work followed by a brisk walk.[2]

Rosa Luxemburg had never been in full agreement with the SPD, and her parting with the party was now beginning. In 1910 she engaged in a public polemic with Kautsky over his reading of the revolution of 1905 and the inapplicability of the mass strike to the Prussian context. The debates over striking as a tactic were one of many in which Rosa showed her resistance towards the trade unions and party officials. This event was the final break between Rosa and the party. Rosa attacked Kautsky over a six-chapter-long pamphlet. The more the party was gaining parliamentary and popular power, the more centre-leaning the party was becoming. Whereas Kautsky was not opposed to strikes in principle, his Marxism was not dialectical and lent further weight towards action through democratic means. At the same time, Kautksy did not see agitation for universal suffrage as central to the present issues. In 1910, a wave of demonstrations and strikes for the cause of universal suffrage had illuminated the revolutionary spirit in the streets.[3] Rosa supported the strikes, viewing them as further strengthening working-class consciousness.[4] It is worth noting here that Rosa continued to be Luise Kautsky's close friend after breaking publicly with her husband. Rosa's spirited psyche, her 'Polish economy', seemed able to reconcile contradictions – she was engaging in ferocious battle with a man while writing affectionate letters to his wife.

Two events had escalated the separation between Rosa and the SPD. When appointing a new chairman in 1911, after the current chairman suddenly died, the SPD found themselves at a crossroads: the choice of either a radical or someone who would collaborate with the Ebert-Schneiderman faction. Both Philip Schneiderman and Friedrich Ebert signalled a clear shift to the right of the party, or rather concessions to right-wing influences that had been bubbling under the surface for a long time. The election of Hugo Haase and Bebel, by now estranged from Luxemburg's politics and position in the party, was a blow to Rosa. Second, in the 1912 election the SPD more than doubled its parliamentary position, making it the largest group in the Reichstag.[5] These moves reshuffled her alliances. The break with Kautsky was complete and beyond remedy, but Franz Mehring became a new and unlikely ally. He had been one of the only supporters of *The Accumulation of Capital* and had become a confidant. Clara Zetkin remained, throughout Rosa's life, a constant comrade to her. Rosa was becoming more and more isolated within the SPD. She was standing at a crossroads, and couldn't foresee the implications of her chosen direction.

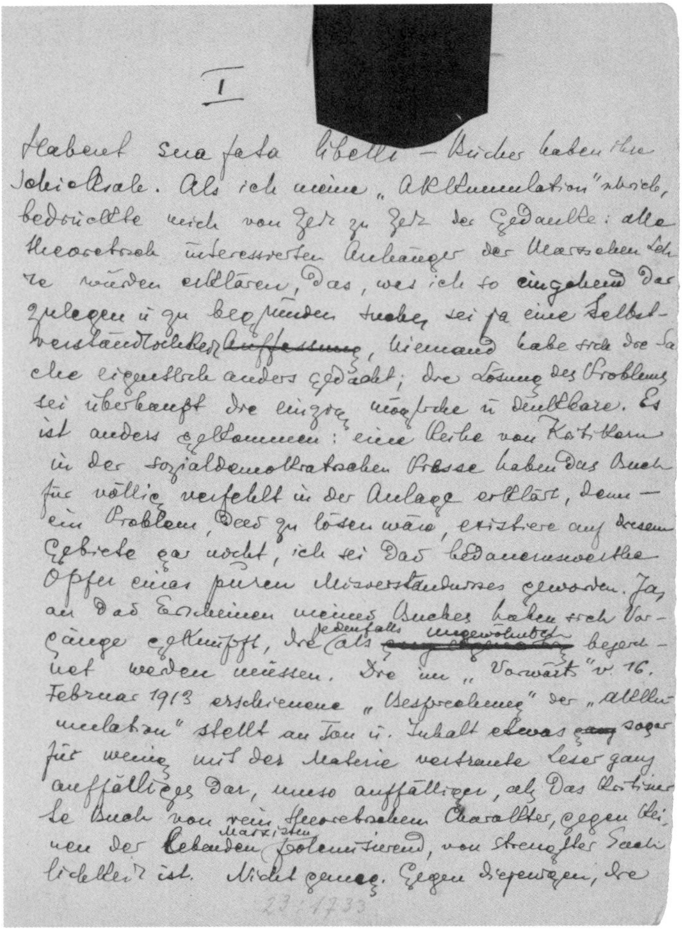

I

[handwritten manuscript in German cursive script]

The first page of the Anti-critique, which Rosa wrote as a response to her critics for the *Accumulation of Capital*. Her four full-length manuscripts were rigorous analytical inquiries into economic structures that underpinned the evil she hated most: global racist capitalism.

Luxemburg's anti-militarism was a consistent strand in her thinking and political agenda. In her article 'The Idea of May Day on the March' (1913), first published in the *Leipziger Volkszeitung*, she wrote:

> The whole development, the whole tendency of imperialism in the last decade leads the international working class to see more clearly and more tangibly that only the personal stepping forward of the broadest masses, their personal political action, mass demonstrations, and mass strikes which must sooner or later open into a period of revolutionary struggles for the power in the state, can give the correct answer of the proletariat to the immense oppression of imperialistic policy. In this moment of armament lunacy and war orgies, only the resolute will to struggle of the working masses, their capacity and readiness for powerful mass actions, can maintain world peace and push away the menacing world conflagration.[6]

In 1911 Rosa had also weighed in on what would become known as the Second Morocco Crisis. The German foreign office was trying to break the alliance between France and England by declaring support for Morocco's sultan, thus splitting the two nations, long-time imperialist rivals in North Africa. The first Moroccan crisis had occurred in 1905; the second was broadly understood to have preceded the tensions that would create the First World War.[7] The International Socialist Bureau, a wing of the International that met between congresses, corresponded on the issue and Rosa, in her role (within her long-standing work in Poland) as representative of SDKPIL, published this internal correspondence. She foresaw that the Morocco affair, which had erupted in July 1911, would be utilized by right-wing parties in elections that year. Rosa responded by publishing a response to the SPD's position, which calmed the critics, and was written by none other than Karl Kautsky.[8] This event signalled a further break with Bebel. Rosa warned that Kautksy's focus solely on election tactics would be dangerous in the SPD's capitulation to the right. In an article published in 1911 she wrote:

> If we are to expect that the Reaction will use Morocco as a decoy to its own advantage, then the only way of making this slogan ineffective and of thwarting this attempt at manipulation is for us to enlighten the masses as soon and as completely as possible as to the deplorable background to the affair and the sordid capitalist interests involved in it.[9]

Further to this, she noted, 'It is not enough for us to rely on the pacific intentions of some capitalist clique as a factor in achieving peace; we can only count on the resistance of the enlightened masses.' She added:

> We have heard so much about the 'splendid situation' in which we are approaching the Reichstag elections, and at the same time we have been warned repeatedly against spoiling this 'situation' by some imprudent action; previously this was the struggle for universal suffrage in Prussia, and now it is the agitation against the hubbub surrounding Morocco.[10]

Putting party strategy over policy was not something Rosa was willing to endorse. Moreover, history would prove her right in fearing the shift of Germany – and the silence of the SPD in the face of this process – towards growing nationalism.

The theoretical enunciation of these conflicts and discussions was published in *Peace Utopias* (1911), in which Luxemburg discussed the difference between the conception of peace brought forth by Centre-Right politicians and her own anti-militarism:

> Our very points of departure are diametrically opposed: the friends of peace in bourgeois circles believe that world peace

and disarmament can be realised within the frame-work of the
present social order, whereas we, who base ourselves on the
materialistic conception of history and on scientific socialism,
are convinced that militarism can only be abolished from
the world with the destruction of the capitalist class state.

Moreover, 'The European states can no longer get along
economically without the non-European countries. As suppliers of
foodstuffs, raw material and wares, also as consumers of the same,
the other parts of the world are linked in a thousand ways with
Europe.'[11] She noted the close links between militarism and colonial
policies and argued that militarism as 'armed peace' was a logical
consequence of capitalism. The only way towards non-weaponized
peace, she argues, is through the proletarian world revolution.
Luxemburg here opposed the idea of the 'united states of Europe' as
an effort to circumscribe militarism. Whereas Europe is a separate
entity geographically, economic struggles within Europe are bound
within extra-European struggles: 'To-day Europe is only a link in
the tangled chain of international connections and contradictions.
And what is of decisive significance – European antagonisms
themselves no longer play their role on the European continent but
in all parts of the world and on all the seas.'[12] We see the connection
between her political agitation and economic analysis exemplified
in *The Accumulation of Capital*. For Rosa, all nations operated within
a global context and must be analysed as such.

She threw scathing critique at Eurocentric views which
discussed peace in Europe:

Every time that bourgeois politicians have championed the
idea of Europeanism, of the union of European states, it has
been with an open or concealed point directed towards the
'yellow peril', 'dark continent', against the 'inferior races',
in short, it has always been an imperialist abortion.[13]

While the Europeans were measuring their histories within self-contained temporalities which championed and celebrated so-called 'peaceful eras', Luxemburg shifts the gaze towards those who have been paying the price in war and violence outside of Europe for those periods. And here we see the continuity of thought of Luxemburg's *Social Reform or Revolution*, asking for determination and commitment to her cause:

> And now if we, as Social Democrats, were to try to fill this old skin with fresh and apparently revolutionary wine, then it must be said that the advantages would not be on our side but on that of the bourgeoisie. Things have their own objective logic. And the solution of the European union within the capitalist social order can objectively, in the economic sense, mean only a tariff war with America, and in the political sense only a colonial race war.[14]

This is an ongoing political battle which she had commenced long ago, and which she was consistently losing. The woman who walked the path of historical dialectics understood that peace cannot be superimposed by political agreements while economic contradictions push towards war. The lifelong hot-headed internationalist refused to refer to her own culture and place of origin as a unique and separate sphere of events. She knew that all events around the globe were playing out in relation to events in Europe.

Unlike her radical, internationalist political outlook, Rosa's cultural tastes were Eurocentric and somewhat conservative. She was a quintessential cultural European who read Goethe, worshipped Mozart and loved Molière, while asking her comrades to understand the world as a whole. She disliked Zola yet read Edgar Allan Poe.[15] She always had a private appreciation for her compatriots Adam Mickiewicz and Frédéric Chopin.[16] In painting, an art she taught and practised successfully herself, she particularly admired the work of the English artist J.M.W. Turner, and his ability to capture light and landscapes.[17] Contradictions were not only played out in the economic-political sphere; they were played within her own Polish economy.

By 1913 the SPD's deputies voted for increased support for a larger military budget.[18] Militarism was now mainstream, and the woman who started her agitation in Germany through the SPD became more and more estranged within its ranks. Her first rival in the SPD, Eduard Bernstein, sought to dismiss her from the party school in 1913, but the students joined forces to oppose this move and the school continued to employ her.[19] In 1914 she met Mathilde Jacob, whose skills as a typesetter would be essential for Rosa's work. On meeting her, Jacob recalled:

> Her large, brilliant eyes which seemed to understand everything, her modesty and goodness, her childish joy at everything beautiful, made my heart beat faster for her. Though often I accompanied her to meetings, conferences or demonstrations, the first impression remained: she looked so modest and unpretentious that people who had not seen her before cried out in amazement: 'that's Rosa Luxemburg?' When she then spoke in her emotional style, she grew beyond her tender little figure and fascinated her listeners.[20]

The overarching sentiment Rosa Luxemburg provoked at first meetings was that of amazement. Her myth preceded her all her life, and yet her charisma and charm allowed Rosa to connect well with other people, many of whom would swiftly become part of her life.

By 1913 Rosa realized that traditionalists within the Social Democratic Party felt that their role was to defend the orthodoxy against any innovation, from either the Right or the Left.[21] Rosa was always a revolutionary, particularly notable within her social democratic circles. The final crisis in the relationship between Rosa and the SPD came in 1914. On 4 August, the SPD, including members Leibknecht and Bernstein, voted in favour of war credits in the Reichstag. And peace within the class war (*Burgfrieden*) was declared – ceasefire in all class struggle.[22] Workers were told to forget about their economic woes. This was an explicit act of support of the imperial German government in its war against the Russian empire, France and Great Britain. This was, contrarily, a vindication of Rosa's worst fears: the victory of capitalism, militarism and imperialism intertwined. The news hit Rosa hard. Yet, never ceasing from action, she hastily organized her first German anti-war meeting, an illegal act. Dissenting against the explicit government and now her own party policy was not only dissident; by her constant anti-military agitation she was breaking the law. Her activism was relentless and sharp:

> Workers! Party comrades! Women of the people! How long will you watch quietly and undisturbed this spectre of hell? How long will you suffer silently the crimes of butchery, need and hunger? Be aware, as long as the people do not move to express their will the genocide will not cease.[23]

After the Reichstag decision, agitation moved beyond the SPD ranks. A splinter group from the SPD referred to itself as the International Group (Gruppe Internationale) after the newspaper *Die Internationale*. From 1916 it started to refer to itself as the Spartacus Group.

On 13 May 1914 Rosa Luxemburg learnt that she was to stand trial for slandering the German army. In her response to the verdict, at a rally at Freiburg in March, she argued that drill and initiation rites were 'torture', 'inhumanity' was endemic in the armed forces. This led to another conviction, this time for insulting the honour of the German officer corps. The proceedings were

A caricature of Rosa's trial, 1914. Clearly she is in power, not the defendant in this depiction. In her life and afterlife she elicited sharp reactions, both admiration and hatred.

joined by Prussian Minister for War Erich von Falkenhayn as associate plaintiff (*Nebenkläger*).[24]

Rosa understood well the politicization of her trial. Rather than a judicial threat, this was a chance for political intervention in the party that, instead of supporting her, had challenged her in the course of the trials and, moreover, had become a dangerous force in an increasingly militarized world. 'What do you think, darling, how fantastic! It's a prosecution from War Minister von Falkenhayn,' she wrote to Paul Levi.[25] History was doing its work and, once more, Rosa was relentlessly doing hers. The trial took place in Berlin between 29 June and 3 July 1914. The break between Rosa and the SPD was no longer theoretical but reality, and she was persecuted for her opinions. But this, in turn, had made her able to intervene forcefully in the political climate that she understood was complicit with evil. The trial became a sphere for the presentation of her ideas, forgoing any attempt at an acquittal. In the speech she gave in Freiburg on 7 March 1914 before the trial, she said:

> a severe criminal stands before you, one condemned by the state, a woman whom the prosecution has described as rootless. Comrades, when I look at this assembly my joy to find here so many men and women of the same opinion is only dimmed by the regret that a few men are missing – the prosecution and the judges of the court in Frankfurt . . . I clearly have better and more solid roots than any Prussian prosecutor.[26]

Rosa of the multiple homelands, who was ostracized within her own political playing field, was, for better or worse, firmly grounded in her ethical and political principles. News of Archduke Franz Ferdinand's assassination on 28 June, the day before Rosa's trial began, pushed bulletins of her trial off the front pages. The vindication of Rosa's views on the harm of war and the decline of humanity and international cooperation would not overjoy anyone in her close circle, not least her. Two public images emerged in parallel from the trial: a martyred, persecuted hero for the anti-war Left; an insidious and unfaithful villain to the Right.

The trial also introduced into Rosa's life another man who would become important to her: Paul Levi. Levi was born on 11 March 1883 to a bourgeois family of assimilated German Jews. His family instilled in him dedication to the arts and democratic values. His passion for socialism and law led him to engage in multiple subjects, from the Dreyfus trial – he retained an admiration for Clemenceau, Dreyfus' defender – to the 'Complaints and Actions against the Administration', the topic of his doctoral thesis in Heidelberg, and a new interpretation of the trial of Socrates he engaged with in the 1920s.[27] At the trial of Rosa Luxemburg, he acted as her lawyer. They also became lovers.

Paul Levi was a different personality to Kostja Zetkin and Leo Jogiches. Levi, a deeply intellectual man and tactician, though less physically striking than Zetkin and Jogiches, was a mature love for Rosa. Gone was the young passion with Leo or the mentoring to Kostja. Letters between Paul and Rosa reveal the great contradiction in her relationships: always failing to find someone of her intellectual and emotional stature yet living passionately within her relationship. As an extraordinary woman she was searching for an equal: 'Darling, it was so nice: on Monday you preached on imperialism in Frankfurt, on Tuesday I did in Charlottenburg.'[28] And yet history would not recall Levi in the same way it did Luxemburg.

Another letter reveals that despite the years that had passed, the trauma of her relationship with Jogiches had not cleared. 'Of all things, the man with mustache [Leo] was here when your telegram arrived. But instinctively I was guarded against mentioning you, and when he asked later whether I was pleased with my attorney, I was guarded with my reply.'[29] In another letter we see the preparations Rosa was making for her inevitable imprisonment: 'I was already prepared for unpleasant decisions. Rosen(feld) and others here believe I may be imprisoned any moment.'[30] This brave spirit, unafraid to take on the German state for her ethics and politics – and pay for it in prison time – remained constantly aware of the dangers of male violence towards women. The contradictions of the life of Rosa Luxemburg are an integral part of her story: the woman who always sought freedom, not only for herself but for all, yet paid a heavy price for the lack of freedom that structural gendered violence brings upon her sex. The gendered element of her arrest is part and parcel of the narrative of her imprisonment.

Upon her arrest, she was not granted her wish to be allowed time to get dressed – instead, her bedroom door was forced open when she was wearing only her nightdress.[31]

Rosa Luxemburg was imprisoned from February 1915 to February 1916. When released, she was greeted by a demonstration of the women who wanted to greet her, the woman who 'we missed so much because she always spoke a sharp word directly to the party leaders, and because she is the kind of person that the people higher up in the party would rather see going *into* prison than coming out of it'.[32] Luise Zietz, the co-founder of International Women's Day together with Clara Zetkin, sent Rosa a telegram of congratulations. Rosa was unequivocally admired as a leader of revolutionary women. She was present when Karl Liebknecht was arrested and 'tried with all the mights of [her] fists to "free" him.'[33] Her own days of freedom did not last long and she was placed in protective custody from July 1916 until 8 November 1918, in a climate of growing hostility towards the revolutionary agitation of which she never ceased. During her prison time she was treated better than other prisoners, received visitations and was allowed food parcels from outside, and yet was attentive to other prisoners' suffering. She had to provide her own food and clothing (Mathilde Jacob notes bringing her underwear) and was allowed to send and receive letters, which would prove a crucial lifeline for her.[34] Specifically, the prison supervisor Frau Stick was taken by the unusual prisoner and showed kindness towards her, once allowing Jacob to bring a bouquet of flowers for her friend Rosa. Alas, Rosa's imprisonments were as subject to turmoil as her life, and she was moved between various facilities, so she did not enjoy this kindness for long. She was transferred from Barnim Street Women's Prison in Berlin to Wronke then Breslau, where she was far more isolated.[35]

Letter writing is a distinct form of writing, it is a genre that is commended independently from theoretical or historical writing, with its own special recognition within the history of literature.

Rahel Varnhagen is known as the most famous Jewish woman of letters, who sent more than 1,000 letters in her lifetime (1771–1833) to her contemporaries, including Heinrich Heine. Rosa was aware of Rahel, as she cites a letter to her in her text 'What Is Political Economy?'[36] Letter writing was a method of exploring the psyche while asking the recipient for candour: this genre of writing demands emotional honesty and an ability for self-revelation, distinct from academic and theoretical work. Rosa's 'Polish economy' is here revealed in its most earnest form to her closest friends and comrades. She began writing letters to her parents and siblings at the age of five, when she first had learnt how to write.[37] In a correspondance of 1898 to Leo she describes walking to post letters as something she 'enjoys tremendously', no doubt combining her twin passions of walking and expressing herself in language.[38] Rosa's letters from prison not only illuminate different sides of her psyche, but exemplify her tremendous writing talent in all forms. Rosa Luxemburg does not feel half way. She throws herself into the depths of emotion with the same vitality that she threw herself into political struggle. But this complex personality includes continuity as well as contradiction. Rosa's letter writing is not distinct from her political work; it should be regarded, as it was by her, as a different genre with its own characteristics.

We gain insight into Rosa's love for the world in the breadth and depth of her letters to her friends while she was imprisoned. The disjuncture between the publicly known, assured comrade Dr Luxemburg and the private Rosa is exposed when considering her letter writing. A woman in the public light, she was cautious in her presentation and yet her relationships were warm and overflowing with kindness and generosity; her letters, though, were never sentimental and one-dimensional, peppered as they were by her unique and spiky sense of humour. Her warmth and caring nature, as well as her own ability for introspection, are always aligned with a relentless concern for justice. Her remarkable intellect allowed her to develop her self-acquired skills in botany and drawing, both of which she practised daily in her prison cell after collecting flowers and plants on her walks. But she was not a hapless romantic; she had a deep understanding of the connections between all injustices. In fact, Rosa's awareness of nature allowed for a very early understanding of environmental justice. It was part of her organic thinking of the world, always as a whole implicated in details, never a mechanic system devoid of humanity.[39] She was often unwell physically and she suffered from depression, yet her writing was incessant. Her interpretation of her gender, her relationships outside of the prison cell and the things that sustained her are all elucidated in her letters from this period.

In December 1916 she wrote to her friend Mathilde Wurm:

> I'm telling you that as soon as I can stick my nose out again I will hunt and harry your society of frogs with trumpet blasts, whip crackings, and bloodhounds – like Penthesilea I wanted to say, but by God, you people are no Achilles. Have you had enough of a New Year's greeting now? Then see to it that you stay human . . . being human means joyfully throwing your whole life 'on the scales of destiny' when need be, but all the while rejoicing in every sunny day and every beautiful cloud. Ach, I know of no formula to write you for being human.[40]

The admiration of nature and environmental activism is intertwined with agitation for humane causes. In another letter, written in 1917, she said:

> For the last few days, wasps have been buzzing into my cell in huge numbers. (Naturally I keep the window open night and day). They come here with a purpose, in search of nourishment, and as you know, I keep open house. I've put out a little bowl for them with all sorts of goodies on it, and

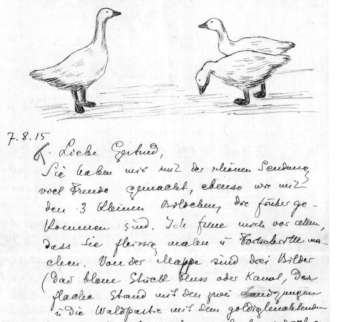

7.8.15

Liebe Gertrud,

Sie haben mir mit der kleinen Sendung viel Freude gemacht, ebenso wie mit den 3 kleinen Bildchen, die früher gekommen sind. Ich freue mich vor allem, dass Sie fleissig malen u. Fortschritte machen. Von der Mappe sind drei Bilder (das blaue Stück Fluss oder Kanal, der flache Strand mit den zwei Landzungen u. die Waldpartie mit dem goldigleuchtenden Himmel) sehr gut; am besten jedoch gefällt mir eins von den winzigen Bildchen: das graue mit d. Fischerbuben; ich finde es ausgezeichnet. So sehr es mir herzlich weh tut, werde ich nächstens mal dieses Bildchen sowie vielleicht das von unserem Ennjuer an Herrn Diefenbach schicken (der mir ungemein wurde), um ihm einen Rippenstoss zu geben. — Aber Sie schreiben ja gar nicht was Sie tre-

Letter from Rosa to Gertrud Zlotko, August 1915, with some drawings. Rosa was a talented yet untrained visual artist, whose artistry showed her holistic understanding of the world as human psyche and nature need more than one outlet.

they busily load themselves up. It's a pleasure to see these tiny creatures disappear out the window every few minutes carrying a new load, betaking themselves to a faraway park, whose green treetops I can barely see off in the distance, and after a few minutes they come flying back in through the window and go right to the bowl. Hanschen, what a fabulous capacity for orientation exists in these little eyes, no larger than a pinhead, and what memory power the wasps have! Day after day they come, and that means that during the night they don't in the least forget the way to that 'fine burgher's lunch table' behind the bars! At Wronke I observed them daily on my walks in the garden, the way they bored deep holes and passageways in the earth between the paving stones, bringing to the surface the dirt they had dug out.[41]

Her compassion extended further:

Take the following episode, which I shall never forget. Last spring I was returning from a country walk when, in the quiet, empty road, I noticed a small dark patch on the ground. Leaning forward I witnessed a voiceless tragedy. A large beetle was lying on its back and waving its legs helplessly, while a crowd of little ants were swarming round it and eating it alive! I was horror stricken, so I took my pocket handkerchief and began to flick the little brutes away. They were so bold and stubborn that it took me some time, and when at length I had freed the poor wretch of a beetle and had carried it to a safe distance on the grass, two of its legs had already been gnawed off . . . I fled from the scene feeling that in the end I had conferred a very doubtful boon.[42]

Rosa's first academic concentration was the natural sciences. Though she later switched to law, she was an enthusiastic botanist all her life; and her time in prison allowed her to develop that strand of interest. These brief snippets from her letters show her understanding of the inextricable link between nature and humanity (which was also apparent when she wrote her text 'Martinique' in 1902) – an understanding she arrived at long before others began to dwell on the relationship between environmental justice and human rights. Rosa acted on behalf of both. She wrote to Sophie Liebknecht in 1917, 'it surprises me a little that Karl wants a book specifically about bird calls. For me the voice of the birds is inseparable from their habitat and their life as a whole, it is only the whole that interests me, rather than any detached detail.'[43] Rosa's letters from prison concerning nature show the intermeshing of solidarity, justice and empathy. She reflected in another letter about an unlikely affinity: 'But I myself am like king Solomon: I too understand the language of the birds, and of all animals.'[44] Rosa's

A tree planted by Rosa while in prison.

empathy extended beyond her human milieu; she understood that idly standing by – choosing not to intervene – while creatures were treated cruelly could create a slippery slope for empathy in society more broadly.

Rosa never felt at home in Berlin, yet as a cultural connoisseur she missed access to her sojourns to the opera and other artistic excursions. She graciously accepted a variety of gifts from friends and comrades (she thanked Rosi Wolfstein, her one-time student, for sending miniatures of two kittens and an elephant for her birthday to adorn her cell)[45] and as ever was concerned about their well-being. Her ever-resilient and creative psyche found a useful alternative to the cultural world she was missing out on while in prison, which she recounted with great joy to Luise Kautsky:

> The great titmice are in loyal attendance in front of my window, they already know my voice exactly, and it seems that they like it when I sing. Recently I sang the Countess's aria from *Figaro*, about six of them were perched there on a bush in front of the window and listened without moving all the way to the end; it was a very funny sight to see. Then there are also two blackbirds that come at my call every day, I've never seen such tame ones. They eat out of the metal plate in front of the window. For this purpose I have ordered a cantata also to be held on April 1 [April fool's day], which should be quite a nice event. Can't you send me some sunflower seeds for these little people?[46]

Rosa refused to bring her cat Mimi with her into prison,[47] since 'the little creature is so accustomed to cheerfulness and liveliness, she likes it when I sing and laugh, and when I play tag with her all over the house, she would definitely get down in the dumps here.'[48] She clarifies that this is a position of empathy and not empty romanticism: 'This is not because, like so many spiritually bankrupt politicians, I seek refuge and find repose in nature. Far from it, in

Rosa's drawing of a bird, ink on *Neue Zeit* paper. Rosa understood the indivisibility of how (wo)man treats nature and their fellow human beings. 'I feel at home in the entire world wherever there are clouds and birds and human tears.'

nature at every turn I see so much cruelty that I suffer greatly.'[49] One instance in which her compassion for the animal kingdom, her anti-militarism and her quest for justice met was during one of her daily walks in the prison courtyard: she encountered buffalo from Romania that were being made to pull a wagon stocked with a load of old army coats from the front, many covered in blood, for the female prisoners to mend and send to the next batch of soldiers being sent into battle. Rosa noticed that the load was so full that the buffalo could no longer pull the wagon. When she asked the soldier in charge of the operation if he had any pity for the animals, he said, 'no one has pity for us humans': 'During the unloading, all the animals stood there, quite still, exhausted, and the one that was bleeding kept staring into the empty space in front of him with an expression on his black face and in his soft, black eyes like an abused child.'[50] Cruelty should not be inflicted on beast or man, and the

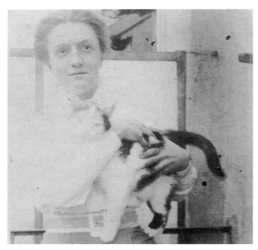

Mimi the cat, held by (possibly) Gertrud Zlotko. This photograph was among Rosa's letters and notes from prison, kept safe while she missed her precious feline friend during her incarceration.

soldier who has no pity for a wounded buffalo would be glad, too, to inflict death upon his fellow man.

The depth of Rosa's ability to empathize with everyone and everything around her created the most significant challenge of her life: to be human, to notice all that surrounded her was afflicted by stark contrasts of beautiful good and terrible evil.

> You ask, 'how does one become good?' 'How does one
> get the "subaltern demon" inside oneself to be quiet?'
> Sonyihcaka,[51] I don't know any way other than to link up
> with the cheerfulness and beauty of life which are always
> around us everywhere, if one only knows how to use one's
> eyes and ears, and thus to create an inner equilibrium
> and rise above everything petty and annoying.[52]

Rosa's understanding of history and time remained unchanged, as she wrote in a letter to another one of her female friends, Martha Rosenbaum, 'dearest, history always itself knows best what to do about things, even when the situation looks most desperate.'[53] The constrained area of the prison cell was a space in which Luxemburg examined the boundaries of her own psyche, continued her work and kept a close eye on current events. She continued to write and develop her political and economic theory and practice. At the same time, the change in Rosa's pace of life allowed her to explore areas of her 'inner Polish economy', and develop her thinking further. Her ability to remain committed to organizing internationally while being away from those she loved most reflects her innate strengths of both self-analysis and self-reflection, a capacity to be highly attentive to her inner voice without neglecting her staunch commitment to the struggle. Rosa loved being on her own and working with strict discipline, without distraction, yet it was always crucial to her to have an attentive listener to engage with through letters – a need most clearly felt during her time in prison. Imprisonment gave Rosa an understanding of the structural nature of wrong as well as right in the world, its oppressions and the way forward to revolution. Her pioneering work included a nascent framework that connected environmental justice with the rights of the oppressed and disabled – her comprehensive understanding of human rights inspired her exploration of her human condition, which she referred to as 'her innermost being'.

Rosa's fourth full-length manuscript, her next large project, was different in essence to the previous three. Her editing and translation of Vladimir Korolenko's *History of My Contemporary*, upon which she worked while incarcerated, stands out in its genre of biography and historical non-fiction, and yet encompasses many ideas at the epicentre of Rosa's work. Her psyche unravelled in the different styles of writing she took on: letters; her economic texts – the zenith of the precision of her analytical mind; and political writing and speeches, which exemplified her passion and ability to galvanize through language. The *Life of Korolenko*, the introduction she wrote to her translation of *History of My Contemporary*, published in 1918, shows her sensitivity to culture and its intimate relationship to political and social change. In a much earlier text ('Stagnation and the Progress of Marxism', 1903), always thinking in dialectics, Rosa stated that 'the proletariat is in a very different position. As a nonpossessing class, it cannot in the course of its struggle upwards spontaneously create a mental culture of its own while it remains in the framework of bourgeois society.'[54] This text analysed the dialectic between the working class and intellectuals with regards to culture:

> In every class society, intellectual culture (science and art) is created by the ruling class; and the aim of this culture is in part to ensure the direct satisfaction of the needs of the social process, and in part to satisfy the mental needs of the members of the governing class . . . The working class will not be in a position to create a science and an art of its own until it has been fully emancipated from its present class position.

This is a sharp observation showing Rosa's understanding that revolution would not arise spontaneously, but instead the revolution would arise from within the logic and progress of history itself; every process will unravel towards the revolution, and the change arises from within the logic of history itself.

The sources appearing in Luxemburg's artistic canon are diverse, though perhaps surprisingly, considering her politics, rather conservative. Schiller, Shakespeare, Cervantes, Dickens, Turner, Markewitz, Poe, Dostoevsky, Gorky and Molière all appear in her writing. Goethe was especially significant for Rosa:

> It was only the music of the words and the strange magic of the poem which lulled me into tranquility. I don't know myself why it is that a beautiful poem, especially by Goethe, so deeply affects me at every moment of strong excitement or emotion. The effect is almost physical. It's

as if with parched lips I were sipping a delicious drink
that cools my spirit and heals me, body and soul.[55]

Luxemburg was attentive to form, and to cultural and historical
histories in relation to both aesthetic and political change. For
Luxemburg it is impossible to disengage the text from the author.
Thus it is essential to look at her own cultural writings in the
context of the map of her own psyche.

Life of Korolenko commences with a powerful quotation: 'my
soul, of a threefold nationality, has at last found a home – and this
above all in the fatherland of Russia.'[56] It proceeds to discuss the
sudden rupture in Russian culture, from 'darkness and barbarism'
to 'something like a miracle', a sudden blossoming of Russian
literature, 'springing up in glistening armor like Minerva from
the head of Jupiter'. Rosa compares the new Russian masters to
many significant literary figures, including Shakespeare, Byron
and Gotthold Ephraim Lessing, and ends her list with her beloved
Goethe. This new literary form, which encompassed many genres
from belles-lettres to contemporary realistic journalism, she
argues, came out of 'an opposition to the Russian regime, out of
the spirit of struggle.'[57] This is not a one-sided process: new art
can emerge from revolutionary moments, but in turn art can spur
revolutionary feelings. As Luxemburg wrote, 'from its first days,
at the beginning of the nineteenth century, it [Russian literature]
never denied its social responsibility – never forgot to be socially
critical.'[58] Luxemburg would never reduce art to propaganda; but
empathy towards another person and the world beyond them,
and the ability to reflect critically on political process – principles
that led her own political work – would become central for her
reflections on culture as well. 'Russian society was gripped with
excitement; writers sounded the alarm.'[59]

The fingerprints of internationalist Rosa are all over this text:
'Turgenev realizes, incidentally, that the first time he fully enjoyed

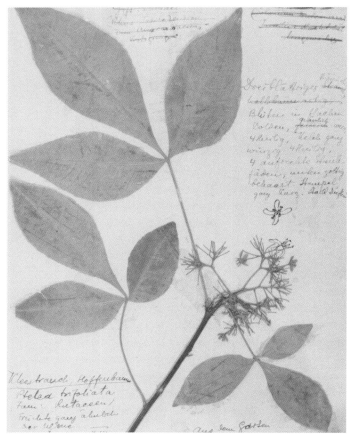

Page from Rosa's Herbarium. Rosa's understanding of the intertwining of man and nature was part of her worldview. 'Larks warble in Russia no less beautifully than in Germany,' she wrote.

the song of the lark he was somewhere near Berlin. This casual remark seems very characteristic. Larks warble in Russia no less beautifully than in Germany.' Later she states:

> what hindered Turgenev from enjoying the beauty of nature in his own country was just that painful disharmony of social relations, that ever present awareness of responsibility for those outrageous social and political conditions from which he could not rid himself, and which, piercing deeply, did not permit for a moment any indulgence in complete self-oblivion.

For Rosa, the world, birdsong, political change and moral responsibility are all intertwined. Later in the text she argues: 'it is just this social sympathy which is responsible for the singularity and artistic splendor of Russian literature.'[60] Art can elicit deep empathy, which gives aesthetic value to a work. Rosa wrote: 'Not only the exceptional person and situation that stands out crassly from the gray background of everyday life, but life itself, the average man and his misery, awakens a deep concern in the Russian writer whose senses are strongly aware of social injustice.'[61] Korolenko wrote in one of his stories that honest human happiness is always elevating to the human soul and man is rather obliged to be happy. Rosa herself understood the root of this statement, once commenting that she was 'cursed to be happy', and, further: 'Happiness makes people spiritually healthy and pure, as sunlight over the open sea effectively disinfects the water.' Moreover, 'Permanent oppression, insecurity, poverty and dependence, as well as that division of labor which leads to one-sided specialization, mold proper in a certain manner. And this goes for both oppressor and the oppressed.'[62] Here we see the indefatigable spirit of Rosa in her analysis, always seeking happiness, and to put order into her own mental state of affairs, her 'Polish economy', as well to see more people around her happy.

Luxemburg spent time discussing Korolenko's fierce anti-death penalty stance. Tolstoy wrote significantly of this intervention:

> your work on the death penalty has just been read to me, and though I tried, I could not hold back my tears. I find no words to express my gratitude and love for a work that is equally excellent in expression, thought, and feeling. It must be printed and distributed in millions of copies. No Duma speeches, no dissertations, dramas, or novels could produce such good results as this work.[63]

Luxemburg herself was ferociously against the death penalty and understood the gravity of this issue. She wrote,

> like his [Korolenko's] articles on the famine and the plague, it contains no set phrases, no hollow pathos. Simplicity and matter of factness prevail throughout. And yet it is outstanding in compassion for human suffering and its understanding of the tottered heart. Exposing the crimes of society which are contained in every death sentence, this little work, full of warmth and highest ethics, became a most stirring accusation.

Luxemburg authored a work entitled 'Against Capital Punishment', published in August 1918:

> Liebknecht and I, on leaving the hospitable halls which we recently inhabited – he, among his pale companions in the penitentiary, I with my dear, poor thieves and women of the streets, with whom I have passed, under the same roof, three years and a half of my life – we took this oath as they followed us with their sad eyes: 'We shall not forget you!'[64]

This is a strong argument showing a deep understanding of the cruelty inherent in the prison system, and the inhumanity of capital punishment. 'Capital punishment, the greatest shame of the ultra-reactionary German code, ought to be done away with at once.'[65] This statement is yet another stance shared between Rosa's time and our own; it is an issue that continues to haunt our own agendas a hundred years after these lines were written. Luxemburg showed how important resisting the death penalty was, as a benchmark for standing in solidarity with humanity as a whole.

The commitment to compassion does not arise from one's own suffering, but rather from the ability to stand in the place of another – to see through their eyes and walk in their shoes. Society's cruelty towards its most vulnerable is telling of its structures of insidious violence. Rosa Luxemburg understood this well. She wrote, 'A world must be turned upside down. But each tear that flows, when it could have been spared, is an accusation, and he commits a crime who with brutal inadvertency crushes a poor earthworm.'[66] Resistance to violence in all its forms, whether towards a beetle, a buffalo or those on the outskirts of society condemned to death, was at the centre of Rosa's understanding of justice.

Especially fascinating is Rosa's focus on the blind musician in Korolenko. Rarely writing about her own disability, a lifelong limp that never stopped her intense walking habit, Rosa's passage here is revealing. We see Rosa's deep compassion as well as her judgement of those who misunderstood her. 'Being born a cripple may be the cause of many conflicts, but is, in itself, beyond all human interference and beyond guilt or vengeance.'[67] 'Living with disability did not grant Luxemburg any special treatment, yet she noticed its omission in other people's narratives.

In literature as well as in art, physical defects are only casually mentioned, either in a sarcastic manner to make an ugly character more loathsome, as Homer's Thersites and the stammering judges in the comedies of Molière and Beaumarchais, or with good-natured ridicule as in genre paintings of the Dutch renaissance, for instance, the sketch of a cripple by Cornelius Dussart. Not so with Korolenko. The anguish of a man born blind and tormented with an irresponsible longing for light is the center of interest.[68]

Rosa was well primed to listen to the voice of Korolenko's blind musician, and more broadly to those multitudes who had been left in the dark or silenced. This passage leads us to think of her own position towards disability: 'today, among the other sparrows that came to eat, was one with a dislocated leg, but he could fly. I felt so sorry for him! All of us kiss you: N.[69] M. and the sparrows.'[70] Elsewhere Mathilde Jacob, Rosa's friend and aide, recounted Luxemburg's help towards a disabled pigeon:

during the winter of 1917–1918 an exhausted pigeon, who could not fly further because of an injured wing, set down on Rosa Luxemburg's cell window. She washed its wound and nursed the little animal until it could fly again. '[T]he brown pigeon' she wrote to me in June 1918, 'which I nursed here in my cell during the winter, when it was ill, remembers my good deed. She discovered me once when I was walking in the yard in the afternoon and now waits punctually for me each afternoon, sits next to me, puffed up, on the pebbles, and runs after me when I go round in a circle. It is comic to see this silent friendship.'[71]

Rosa's friendliness to the animal kingdom was a consequence of her understanding of the intertwining of nature and humanity, especially as a person with a disability herself, as well as her attentiveness to all those, human and non-human, whose march towards liberty and equality needed further help. We can see this attentiveness as a burgeoning crusade to understand disability rights. Justice and empathy were always one for Rosa.

Korolenko's book is an impressive unfolding of his childhood: his impressions of his parents, descriptions of various historical tribulations of the era, reflections on education, his political estimation of 'autocratic Russia', and thoughts on the cultural landscapes of St Petersburg and Moscow. There is specific discussion of the process of his arrest and consequent exile, and he ends his text with a note on populism. The rigorous work covers the reign of Alexander II, both as a personal history and an observer's snippet. Rosa concluded her introduction to Korolenko's *History of My Contemporary*: 'sociality and solidarity with the misery of men means salvation and enlightenment for the individual as well as for the masses.' She then pointed out, 'In Eastern Europe the subject most preferred for diverting the people's bad disposition has always been the Jews, and it is questionable whether they have yet played their role to the end.'[72] Rosa highlighted Korolenko's solidarity with her own people, the Jews, in the face of the trials over a Jewish murder case of 1913, in which Menahem Beilis, a Russian Jew, was accused of ritual murder in Kiev. This argument allows for another reflection into Luxemburg's relationship to her own Jewishness. In the same way that Rosa appreciated Korolenko extending solidarity to her own people, she extended her solidarity to people across the world, in countries she never even visited but she knew carried the brunt of suffering as a result of injustice.

Perhaps the depth of the human psyche is most revealed when it surprises itself. The cocky Rosa, who was not afraid to take on some of the most established figures on the German Left as a Jewish émigré from Poland, at the age of 27, was taught the hardest lesson about the limits of her humanity and the generosity of humanity itself towards her some twenty years later, when she was vindicated in the worst way imaginable. Hanschen, her beloved

Hans Diefenbach, with whom she had conducted a long-distance love affair, mainly through letters, was one of those men whose blood-stained garments were carted from the battlefield, as he lost his life in the First World War. Diefenbach was a physician who advocated for the SPD's goals. In 1917, he was killed in action, at the age of 33. Rosa's grief was profound. She reminisced that 'Hans, like a child with tears in his eyes, protested to us that he did not want to and could not go to war, [and that] he had a feeling he would not return, [and] now I had to comfort him like a little child.'[73] Rosa spent her life agitating so that no human being would lose loved ones as a consequence of militarism and war. And here she was, paying that dear emotional price. 'Actually I am living in a dream world in which he is not dead. For me he lives on, and I often smile when I think about him.'[74] Rosa was always a realist visionary and certainly never chose to escape reality, but in this case reality was hard to bear. Her resistance to the war sent her behind bars; the war cost the life of her beloved Hans. Nevertheless, her generosity of spirit sustained her, even in this darkest hour: 'in me he continues to live.'[75]

Rosa Luxemburg and her comrades had long parted ways before the formal founding of the Spartacus League in 1916. However, its foundation made her and her co-founders, Clara Zetkin, Franz Mehring and Karl Liebknecht, de facto leaders. These were her closest comrades-in-arms at this time. Other prominent members were, among others, Julian Marchlewski, Wilhelm Pieck and Bertha Thalheimer. The official founding of the Spartacus League transformed Rosa from a left-wing outlier to a leader. One of her most famous texts, the *Junius Pamphlet*, written anonymously in 1915, was a blasting outcry against the complex and lasting consequences of war. Luxemburg's writing during the war years was urgent, explosive and poignant.

The *Junius Pamphlet* must be read in the context of other works around that time. In another essay, published in *Die Internationale*,

'Rebuilding the International' (1915), Luxemburg connected the start of the First World War with the collapse of the International (in a letter from 1914 she had written that 'the party and the International have gone kaput'),[76] and that 'the collapse of the International is complete as it is dreadful!'[77] Furthermore, she elucidated 'the disastrous self-deception of the socialist parties' that led to making the socialist International 'a fiction, a hypocrisy'.[78] She continued to state that the alternatives were clear: 'socialism or imperialism' – where German social democracy took over imperialism on the battleground. She criticized the social democratic women who found time to support men fighting on the frontline. The woman question for Rosa was always bound up in larger issues. She continued by discussing the significance of international solidarity in times of war. She supplied a clear-cut presentation of the dilemma:

> either the class struggle is the paramount law of existence of the proletariat, and the party officials' proclamation of class harmony in its place during war-time is an outrage against the proletariat's vital interests; or the class struggle in both war and peace is an outrage against the 'national interests' and 'the security of the fatherland'.

She concluded that 'the only real safeguard for peace depends on the resolution of the proletariat to remain faithful to its class politics and its international solidarity through all the storm of imperialism.'[79] The dictum goes: either imperialism or socialism. To retain the power of the International, one must take a road 'that is not paved with resolutions' but at the same time is 'the road to peace'. The *Junius Pamphlet* presented an interesting shift in Rosa's position on national self-determination, affirming that socialism alone can achieve it for peoples in either war or peace. This was not a full concession on her position on nationalism, but rather acceptance of nationalism within socialist tactics. Nonetheless this is one area in which she was ostensibly behind the march of history, reaching the position of Marx and Engels in the 1860s.[80] The year 1914 shattered much of Luxemburg's philosophy, but it also crystallized differences between herself and the leading Marxists of her time, Lenin and Kautsky. Until 1914, Kautsky, as the chief interpreter of Marxism in the national question,[81] equated the national interest with that of the proletariat; gaining national emancipation would benefit the working classes. Luxemburg, however, subsumes one in the other; the revolution is always the first focus of action, not national emancipation.[82]

In late 1915, Rosa wrote her *Theses on the Tasks of International Social-Democracy*, in which she traced the path by which the start of the world war had annihilated the work of forty years of European socialism, as a result of the leaderships betraying the interests of the working classes. In an era of unleashed imperialism, there was no such thing as a national war. No longer could a single country gain liberty and independence. World peace would not emerge from utopian projects or reactionary moves of capitalist diplomats. She returned to her thesis from *The Accumulation of Capital*, arguing that imperialism follows from the expansion of capital and as such is the enemy of the proletariat. Here we see Rosa's perfect melding of theory and practice. The International, she affirms, is the centre of action and must take precedence. National language is a way through which bourgeois tutelage expresses itself and the mission of socialism is to enable the spiritual emancipation of the proletariat from that onus.[83] The workers' fatherland is the socialist International.

The *Junius Pamphlet* was named after Junius, a pseudonym for a letter writer who wrote on the infringement of civil rights and the duty the English government had towards its citizens in the eighteenth century. Luxemburg begins by discussing the change in the international scene. The world war was a global drama. Its dramatic tone frames one of her most forceful quotes:

> Shamed, dishonored, wading in blood and dripping with
> filth, thus capitalist society stands. Not as we usually see
> it, playing the roles of peace and righteousness, of order, of
> philosophy, of ethics – but as a roaring beast, as an orgy of
> anarchy, as a pestilential breath, devastating culture and
> humanity – so it appears in all its hideous nakedness.[84]

As is noticeable in this text, Rosa's style was achieving new heights,
her urgency expressed in a more dramatic discourse.

The crux of the argument commences early, when Rosa
states that democracy has capitulated. The emphasis, as in any
text Luxemburg wrote, was on whether or not the proletariat's
consciousness could transcend to the next historical level:
'socialism is lost only if international proletariat is able to measure
the depths of the catastrophe and refuses to understand the lesson
it teaches.'[85] Even during one of the darkest hours for humanity,
as the consequent analysis shows, Luxemburg placed her hope for
transformation on the consciousness of the masses. The zenith of
the international struggle, and thus the pinnacle of capitulation,
was German social democracy. Thus the analysis starts with
its fall. The way to challenge crises is to intervene in their
development and crystallization of what is considered possible in
order to build a new consciousness for the masses, the core goal of
Luxemburg's work:

> while capitalist society, shamed and dishonored, rushes
> through the bloody orgy to its doom, the international
> proletariat will gather the golden treasures that were
> allowed to sink to the bottom in the wild whirlpool of the
> world war in the moment of confusion and weakness.[86]

The world war was a turning point, an opportunity to thrust
forward the case of the proletariat.

Luxemburg moves from this to a clear presentation of the dialectic between historical necessity and agency: 'scientific socialism has taught us to recognize the objective laws of historical development. Man does not make history of his own volition, but he makes history nonetheless.'[87] This is a direct reference to Marx, who wrote in *The Eighteenth Brumaire of Louis Napoleon* that 'men make their own history, but they do not make it as they please', yet elucidates Luxemburg's clear reception of the dialectical idea. Her faith in the cause of socialism was unwavering:

> The proletariat is dependent in its actions upon the degree of righteousness to which social evolution has advanced. But again, social evolution is not a thing apart from the proletariat; it is the same measure, its driving force and its cause as well as its product and its effect. And though we can no more skip a period in our historical development than a man can jump over his shadow, it lies within our power to accelerate or retard it.

We cannot change the march of history, but it is up to us – as each and every one of us is part of the masses, that great engine which pushes the march of history along – to do *our* work: 'socialism is the first popular movement in world history that has set itself the goal of bringing human consciousness, and thereby free will, into play in the social actions of mankind.' Rosa claims to quote Friedrich Engels, who stated that bourgeois society stands at the crossroads, either transition to socialism or regression into barbarism.[88] Luxemburg reframed and elucidated the crossroads of her own march: the march of German social democracy and history is placed between socialism and imperialism. She wrote: 'We are like the Jews whom Moses led through the desert. But we are not lost and we will be victorious if we have not forgotten how to learn.'[89] The tenacity and resilience of the Jewess whose march was never halted, and her never-ending passion to transform consciousness and to agitate to action, are the red thread of both the *Junius Pamphlet* text and her life's work. The promised land of socialism awaited those always moving towards it.

The concession of social democracy to militarism marked the shift into the present stage of crisis. Her polished theoretical analysis was immediately transformed into a political outcry. Luxemburg denounced the government's forcing of the opposition press to capitulate to its opinion. The stifling of press freedom was intimately related to the concessions to the working-class struggle. This in turn strengthened the war under the guise of civil peace. Here we see again the two pillars of Rosa Luxemburg's writings: Marxism and democracy. This text encapsulates many avenues of critique: anti-militarism, anti-imperialism, anti-colonialism, the ruin of nature (in understanding the ruining of agricultural land as intertwined in violence towards human beings), and of course the underlying structure, socialism. It is crucial to separate these categories analytically from each other and see how the lines of critique resonate and highlight the urgency of Rosa's calls for action. At the same time, this text exemplifies the need to resist all oppressions simultaneously. Here we return to the woman who felt compassionate for the suffering buffalo carrying blood-stained cloth returning from the war; the woman who understood, viscerally, that oppressions cannot be compartmentalized. Rosa's empathy towards the suffering buffalo, and, in turn, towards the countless dead soldiers whose blood was dripping from the bourgeoisie's hands led to this rallying cry for action.

Luxemburg shifted to what would be the culmination of the argument: there can be no nationalistic wars of self-defence.

Capitalist politicians, in whose eyes the rulers of the people and the ruling classes are the nation, can honestly speak of the 'right of national self-determination' in connection with such colonial empires. To the socialist, no nation is free whose national existence

is based upon the enslavement of another people, for to him
colonial people too are human beings, and, as such, part of the
nation state. International socialism recognizes the right of free
independent nations, with equal rights. But socialism alone can
create such nations, can bring self-determination of their peoples.[90]

According to Rosa Luxemburg, as long as there is imperialism
there can be no 'national self-determination' either in war or in
peace. Capitalism is international and hence the resistance to it
must be international. Those who claim themselves oppressed
within European capitalism are actually the oppressors within
imperialism. The right of national self-determination should be
demanded against the imperialist war only.

Luxemburg's motivation was always the call for action.
'Revolutions are not "made" and great movements of the people
are not produced according to technical recipes that repose in the
pockets of the party leaders.'[91] The dialectic between spontaneous
uprisings and organization is enunciated by quoting her own text
from 1906, *The Mass Strike, Political Party and Trade Unions*. Action
and determinate narratives of history always act in dialectic.

> The voice of our party would have acted as a wet blanket
> upon the chauvinistic intoxication of the masses. It
> would have preserved the intelligent proletariat from
> delirium, would have it more difficult for imperialism
> to poison and stupefy the minds of the people.

Imperialism is the catalyst; social democracy is the object in crisis.
But the masses are always the subject able to progress it to the next
stage. The masses are always the agents of change despite being the
subjects of social democracy. Notwithstanding infringement on
civic and democratic freedoms, a new class solidarity arises from
the bloody battlefields.

The *Junius Pamphlet* concluded with a call for future-orientated organizing. Moving away from present-based discussions of victory/defeat, she argued explicitly: 'the class conscious proletariat cannot identify with any of the military camps in this war. The dialectic moves the march of history into the next step. The push towards strengthening the proletariat is this text's narrative and Rosa's life's work. 'The world war is a turning point. For the first time, the ravening beasts at loose upon all quarters of the globe by capitalist Europe have broken into Europe itself.' Rosa critiqued the passivity of European states towards horrors occurring to the people of Herero and in the Kalahari, China, Tripoli and on the Putumayo River under the guise of 'a world war'. Rosa's internationalism was grounded in universal compassion, in understanding the fact that everyone's fate, and hence that of humanity as a whole, is closely bound together. The woman who was able to consider the full-scale cruelties of the Great War simply by witnessing a buffalo loaded with blood-soaked rags understood that empathy itself was a powerful force forged by the human imagination. The imagination must be unleashed through agitation. The end of the text reads as a harrowing cry to those who will outlive Rosa. She warns against the nationalism of the cries 'Deutschland, Deutschland über alles'.[92] At the end of the 1906 revolution, Rosa wrote: 'the revolution is magnificent – all else is bilge!'[93] The arc of history would bend in a way not even Rosa could foresee. And yet, she ends the *Junius Pamphlet*, ever agitating, ever thinking of a better day, reiterating Marx's dictum: 'Proletarians of all lands, Unite!'

5

Ultimate Revolutionary Duty

'The whole of Europe is filled with the spirit of revolution,' remarked Lloyd George to the French Premier Clemenceau in March 1919; the years 1917–19 were especially so.[1] Revolutions have many different meanings. They involve unerring, daily commitment to the idea that 'another world is possible', and are bolstered by elaborate political programmes; they try to realize ethical ideals and act as ruptures in the narratives of history – moments in which dissent and horizons of hope unveil themselves. Revolution energized Rosa's theory and practice throughout her life. A momentous revolutionary moment was about to unfold, and she was not going to be barred from it, even if she was still behind physical bars.

The strife that sparked the 1905 revolution in the Russian empire had not disappeared, and the suffering of the hungry masses had escalated. Russia's losses in the First World War – the massive size of its army was negated by its archaic fighting strategies – took large tolls on its society and economy, notably creating shortages of food and coal, thereby heightening the prices of both. As the tsar's rule became more and more authoritarian, the masses resented the lack of civil and political rights and the economic and social strife. Then, in one instant, the spark that transformed world history forever was lit. Adding to the unrest, hunger and strikes of the time, especially of female garment workers, who had been the engines of unrest in 1896 and then in 1905, riots began to spread. This was the start of the Russian Revolution of 1917. The tsar appointed an intermediary government, which included a young lawyer named Alexander Kerensky, who became a prominent vice minister and later Prime Minister. At the same time, radical organizing continued relentlessly. The workers formed soviets (organized local workers' councils) and took control of government buildings.

Kerensky, leading a liberal line in the new political constellation as Minister of War, released political prisoners and advocated freedom of speech. However, the workers and farmers, disenfranchised and poor despite these changes, gained little tangible outcomes from these political reforms. The personality who would be most remembered from these events and would indeed become the peoples' guiding light at the time was writing from afar when the revolution broke out. On the night of 3 April 1917 Lenin stepped off the train in Finland Station, St Petersburg. He arrived to take charge of the fledgling revolution. After attacks on the Bolsheviks from Kerensky's government, Lenin insisted on action to be taken before the election of the Russian Constituent Assembly after the February revolution. On 26 October 1917, the Second All-Russian Congress of Soviets handed over power to the Soviet Council of People's Commissars. Lenin was elected chairman.

Orders were given for the Bolsheviks to occupy the railway stations, the telephone exchange and the state bank. The following day the Red Guards surrounded the Winter Palace. Inside was most of Russia's government cabinet, although Kerensky had managed to escape from the city. As chairman of the Council of People's Commissars, Lenin abolished private ownership of land and began distributing it among the peasants. Banks were nationalized and Lenin introduced workers' control of factory production. Lenin's political programme was outlined in the ten April Theses, which would be the blueprint of the revolution.[2] Russia was in transition from the first, bourgeois, stage of the revolution to its proletarian stage. The soviets may have been a minority, Lenin recognized, but were necessary for the transformation between the stages. A parliamentary republic, he warned, would swiftly return to a monarchy. He called for the abolition of the police, army and bureaucracy, control over public officials' salaries and nationalization of all land, as well as the creation of one, national, central bank. Lenin proposed that instead of introducing socialism as an artificial product imposed from above, the first step needed to be strengthening the control of soviets. With regard to the Bolshevik Party, Lenin demanded a 'commune state' and amendment of the party programme. Lastly and crucially, he called for a new International. He wrote forcefully: 'At a time of revolution, when the imperialist world war is in progress, we cannot stand still.'[3]

The second Russian Revolution was important to Rosa intellectually and emotionally. Her first response was unwavering solidarity, and delight at progress:

> You can imagine what a turmoil [the news from] Russia has stirred within me. So many old friends who have been languishing in prison for years in Moscow, in St Petersburg, Orel or Riga are now walking around free. How much that lightens the burden for me sitting here! . . . I am content with it and do not begrudge them their freedom even if my chances have become so much the worse as a direct result.[4]

Rosa's immersion in the revolution was personal, organizational and theoretical, with those aspects often hard to untangle from each other; through everything the concept of freedom remained central and galvanizing. As a woman who saw socialism as the way to emancipate humankind as a whole, Rosa understood this was a watershed moment. She also understood its international origins and implications:

> for a week or so my thoughts have of course been on St Petersburg. With impatient hands both morning and evening

I seize on the latest newspapers, but of course the news is meagre and confused. Lasting success there is certainly not to be counted on, but in any event the courage to seize power is itself a punch in the face for Social Democracy here and for the whole slumbering International.[5]

At the same time, Rosa also understood that the scope of history transcends any individual event, as monumental as it may be. Thus success and failure are not to be hastily declared from the battleground:

the events in Russia are of amazing grandeur and tragedy. Lenin and his people will not of course be able to win against the insuperable tangle of chaos, but their attempt, by itself, stands as a deed of world-historical significance and a genuine milestone . . . I am sure that the noble German proletarians, just like the French and English workers, will at the present time all look on while the Russians bleed to death.[6]

Before the revolution broke up Luxemburg exhibited a clear theoretical understanding of the dialectics of history, presented in a nutshell in a fond personal letter to her friend Martha Rosenbaum: 'Dearest, history itself always knows best what to do about things, even when the situation looks most desperate.'[7]

Trotsky celebrated his 38th birthday when the Bolsheviks seized power, on 7 November, and whereas he had had ideological conflicts with Lenin in the past, he joined the Bolshevik Party just before the 1917 revolution and supported Lenin's one-party line during the revolution. Trotsky was the founder of the Red Army, Commissar of War and in many ways the organizer most opposite to Lenin's ideologue. Despite crossing paths with him several times, Rosa never felt affectionate towards Trotsky, and found nothing creditable in him.[8]

In April 1917, as Lenin was taking his first steps into the revolution in St Petersburg, Luxemburg wrote in a piece entitled 'The Old Mole':

> The outbreak of the Russian Revolution has broken the stalemate in the historical situation created by the continuation of the world war and the simultaneous failure of the proletarian class struggle. For three years Europe has been like a musty room, almost suffocating those living in it. Now all at once a window has been flung open, a fresh, invigorating gust of air is blowing in, and everyone in the room is breathing deeply and freely of it.[9]

Always the internationalist, Luxemburg focused her attention both on the effects beyond Russia, in Germany, and on international exchanges that occur away from faux peace agreements signed on the backs of starving workers. She was never bright-eyed about the challenges of the revolution and yet recognized its significance within history, the giant leap it had been for so many, repeating her maxim from the *Junius Pamphlet*:

> Old mole. History, you have done your work well! At this moment the slogan, the warning cry, such as can be raised only in the great period of global change, again resounds through the International and the German proletariat. That slogan is: Imperialism or Socialism! War or Revolution! There is no third way![10]

The masses were always the revolutionary subject, always the locus of democracy. In 1905 Rosa had declared that the revolution was in the good hands of the Russian proletariat. The 1917 Russian Revolution would be the event in which Luxemburg would enunciate more clearly her commitment to democracy as essential in the revolutionary process. Her belief in the ability to create revolution and socialism from the ground up, and her deep understanding of how historical processes unfolded, continued throughout her life's work. 'The masses are always what they must be according to the circumstances of the times, and they are always on the verge of becoming something totally different from what they seem to be.'[11] The commitment to and faith in 'the masses', which can otherwise be stated as her commitment to revolutionary democracy, was clearly articulated in her work *The Russian Revolution*, which created a stir at the time of its writing, 1918, and for many years after its publication in 1922.

Rosa's jubilant start to the pamphlet sets the tone of the piece:

> The Russian Revolution is the mightiest event of the World War. Its outbreak, its unexampled radicalism, its enduring consequences, constitute the clearest condemnation of the lying phrases which official Social-Democracy so zealously supplied at the beginning of the war as an ideological cover for German imperialism's campaign of conquest.[12]

She quickly critiqued Kautsky and others in the SPD, arguing that if there is a discrepancy between the revolutionary consciousness and the unravelling of history, that is the mistake of the leaders, not the revolution and the masses.[13] Her break with the SPD mainstream Right was consolidated and her loyalties realigned. In a letter to Mehring a year before writing *The Russian Revolution* she commented, with characteristic humour, 'With one eye laughing and the other eye weeping I am following the inexhaustible outpouring of Kautsky's pen.'[14]

Always an internationalist, Luxemburg understood that this event transcended its immediate area of eruption. She continued to argue that Lenin and Trotsky had taken a decisive step, one which should be seriously regarded by the Second International.[15] Rosa saw the capitulation of her SPD comrades to war and centrism as the death of the International. Since the SPD was the largest party and had moved itself to the Centre-right, it meant that the International had little hope to be a socialist unifying body. The Russian Revolution, she understood immediately, was a way to bring together those entrenched in the struggle towards peace and socialism in theory and practice. From Marx's own work through the first revolution, the force of events in Russia had always been of significance for the entire world. Rosa defended the constituent assembly and universal suffrage in sharp opposition to Lenin and Trotsky's position.[16]

From here she proceeds to one of the passages most central to her canon as well as to receptions of the Russian Revolution: "'Thanks to the open and direct struggle for governmental power," [she quotes from Trotsky], "the laboring masses accumulate in the shortest time a considerable amount of political experience and advance quickly from one stage to another of their development.'"[17] According to Luxemburg, Trotsky presents an irresolvable tension: on the one hand, the belief that public life is crucial for the development of the revolutionary process (with which she agreed), and on the other, organizational tendencies that moved to circumscribe public debate and participation (of which she was highly critical).

It is the very giant tasks which the Bolsheviks have undertaken with courage and determination that demand the most intensive political training of the masses and the accumulation of experience. Freedom only for the supporters of the government, only for the members of one party – however numerous they may be – is no freedom at all. Freedom is always and exclusively freedom for the one who thinks differently. Not because of any fanatical concept of 'justice' but because all that is instructive, wholesome and purifying in political freedom depends on this essential characteristic, and its effectiveness vanishes when 'freedom' becomes a special privilege.[18]

The text contains many enthusiastic endorsements of both revolution as ethos and the Russian Revolution in particular. But it also contains three lines of critique, which have been remembered more than the revolutionary spirit in which the text was written and which spills over from every line. First, Luxemburg argues against Lenin's endorsement of the right for self-determination as a national liberty within the revolutionary struggle. This was a lifelong commitment that she had held on to, however wrong history had proven her; and at this stage she had enough signs to see on which side of history she was. At the same time, writing about this in 1918, the concept of self-determination had gained a different context as Stalin had already redefined Lenin's thesis and rearticulated it 'almost as a caricature of RL'[19] – 'all this leads to the necessity of interpreting the principle of self-determination not as a right for the bourgeoisie but exclusively for the working masses of the nation concerned. The principle of self-determination must be an instrument in the struggle for socialism and must be subordinated to the principles of socialism.'[20] Second, Luxemburg attacked the distribution of land rather than its nationalization – her preferred choice. The third line of Luxemburg's critique was the one most remembered from the pamphlet and which has caused the most debate in her afterlife. The central question she raises is the critical nature of and control over a revolution, or, in other words, the dialectic between the masses, the proletariat and a central directive power.[21] The Bolsheviks dissolved the constituent assembly, which had only met for thirteen hours before being dismantled in January 1918. It was substituted by the Third All-Russian Congress of Soviets. Thus an elected body was replaced by an unelected one. Together with the question of suffrage, this was key for Luxemburg's critique of the Bolsheviks, and yet cannot simply be read as positing her as an 'anti-Leninist', as many have done in her life and after. Democratic orientation was the start and the central point of critique for Luxemburg.[22] Once again she returned to the fact that for her, unequivocally, the masses are the subject and bearers of the revolution: 'The whole mass of the people must take part of it [that is, the development of a socialist society]. Otherwise, socialism will be decreed from behind a few official desks, by a dozen intellectuals.'[23]

This is not only a logically coherent argument within the text, but a direct culmination of an argument she pursued throughout her life, from 'Organizational Questions of Russian Social Democracy' (1904), through to *Mass Strike* (1906) and the *Junius Pamphlet* (1915). Throughout her political life Rosa defended freedom of speech and the theory and practice of revolutionary democracy, from her earliest days joining the Proletariat, a Polish party which had seen its leaders hung, to her own price paid in incarceration for standing up to her capitulating party. Conceptually the pamphlet addresses and continues a problem discussed by Marx and Engels and those they inspired, namely how to mobilize the non-revolutionary proletariat.[24] Her lifelong belief was that the proletariat would attain revolutionary consciousness by itself; thus she rejected the idea of utilizing a revolutionary minority that would impose political myth on the working class. Socialism would come from below or it would not be socialism at all.[25]

The revolution is bound in social democracy, and social democracy, for Rosa, is understood and practised through freedom as an idea and process. The suppression of dissent cannot be justified as a necessary evil in order to attain the final revolutionary goal, yet we should remember Rosa's entrance to the SPD's stage seventeen years earlier, when she emphasized that 'the final goal was everything.' The Russian Revolution is both in form and content an enunciation of freedom and democracy within the Marxist revolutionary tradition, which really is the luminous point of the Russian Revolution. Rosa felt personally implicated in the revolution. An internationalist through and through, she knew the

German working class would be influenced by events across their borders, regardless of whether or not the people would take action in their own land.

On 3 November 1918, a mutiny of sailors and workers in Kiel marked what would become known as the German Revolution. Jan Valtin, a fellow Spartacist, recalled: 'That night I saw the mutinous sailors roll in to Bremen in caravans of commandeered trucks – red flags and machine guns mounted on the trucks.'[26] A sailor recalled:

> Rumors circulated to the effect that it had been decided to engage the army in a final encounter, in which the German fleet would triumph or die for the glory of the 'Kaiser and the Fatherland'; when they met they saluted one another with 'long live Liebknecht'. The population was in the streets. From all sides masses of humanity, a sea of swinging, pushing bodies and distorted faces was moving toward the centre of the town. Many of the workers were armed with guns, with bayonets, with hammers.[27]

Forty-nine sailors were arrested in Kiel after the failed insurrection; they had refused to abide by a new government in which the leader of the SPD, Philip Schneiderman, was a minister. The uprising had been provoked by an armistice with the British, in which the German navy was under order to destroy its own fleet. By the end of the day, the city was under the control of the insurgent revolutionaries. The insurgence spread to Hamburg, Hanover, Frankfurt and Munich. On 9 November the revolutionaries took hold of Rosa Luxemburg's lifelong adopted home city, Berlin. The imperial government handed its power to the social democrats in a government led by Ebert. The Kaiser abdicated. The Reichstag was occupied by Revolutionary Stewards, a grassroots' workers party. Midday saw the declaration by Schneiderman from the Reichstag – despite not having the backing of all SPD officials – of Germany as a republic. At 4 p.m., to a crowd of equal size to the one attending Schneiderman's declaration, Rosa's recently released comrade Karl Liebknecht declared a 'free socialist republic of Germany' and raised the red flag of the republic.

On the night of 9 November Rosa was released from prison. She walked out of it a changed woman. Her hair had turned white; her health had deteriorated as a result of repeated bouts of illness. She was not the young radical who marched into Berlin in 1898, but her revolutionary energy still quickened with every step she took. Her journey from prison towards the burgeoning revolution was on an overcrowded train, sitting on a suitcase between passengers and luggage.[28]

Rosa Luxemburg and Karl Liebknecht were aware of death threats targeting them when they were thrust back into the world of Berlin politics. As she wrote to Clara Zetkin:

> every few days come urgent warnings from 'official sources'
> that Karl and I are threatened by gangs of killers, so that
> we are not supposed to sleep at home but must seek shelter
> somewhere else, until the point was reached that this business
> became so stupid, in my opinion, and I simply came back here
> to Sudense. I have been living this way, in the midst of tumult
> and turmoil and all in a rush from the first moment, and I
> don't have time to come to my senses or get my bearings.[29]

Rosa and Karl got back to work immediately, writing, agitating and organizing though they knew well their lives were at risk. They began to publish the newspaper *Die Rote Fahne* (the Red Flag), conceptualized as the organ of the working class.[30] Rosa had worked in publishing throughout her life; from her early years at the *Gazeta Robotnicza* she understood and worked ceaselessly to get radical ideas heard. It was a boon to Rosa to have friends, such as

Mathilde Jacob, who were skilled in typesetting – this provided her with an opportunity for collaboration as well as friendship.

After her release from prison Rosa was constantly on the move. In a letter from November 1918 she wrote under the location Hotel Moltke, 'my address for now'.[31] In a letter from 2 November 1918 to Clara Zetkin she wrote, 'write something perhaps about women, that is so important now, and none of us here understand anything about it.'[32] Women were integral to the Russian Revolution, and Rosa always understood that analysing the force of women within Russia's uprising was crucial for the progression of the German movement too. For her feminism was always enacted both in theory and in practice, especially collaborations with her close women comrades. The woman question was always bound in larger historical processes, and for Rosa, the revolution – as the peak of the development of economic-political history – was a

Clara Zetkin and Rosa Luxemburg walking together, n.d., before 1919 (third woman unidentified, possibly Gertrud Zlotko). Clara was the recipient of a letter found in Luxemburg's handbag when she was murdered.

prime time to examine revolutionary feminism. Her release from prison certainly marked a change in Rosa's relationship to her own perception of the woman question, which became much more paramount as a central topic for agitation. This letter to Clara again testifies that she is staying with the always trustworthy Mathilde Jacob, and 'I still haven't been home' appears under her address. Upon leaving her cell and re-entering society, Rosa understood more fully an existential homelessness, which was now experienced by people every day on a vast scale. Her hope for revolution remained alive in her letters, even when the failings and fight back of the German revolution were already in full swing.

Rosa's attitude towards a revolution in Germany – a cause for which she had agitated all her life – was, from the revolution's surprising outbreak, far more cautious and measured than that of the Russian counterpart. She understood the constraints of the eruption and development of the events in their specific historical and social context. In *Oh! How German is this Revolution!*, an aptly cynical title, she wrote:

> For the political victims of the old regime of reaction we ask neither 'amnesty' nor mercy. We demand the right of freedom, fight and revolution for those hundreds of true and faithful men and women who are languishing in jails and prisons because they dared to fight for liberty, for peace and for Socialism under the rule of the sword of the imperialistic criminals whose rule has now come to an end.

But, she clarifies, it was not the Schneiderman socialists to whom the revolution was indebted. As ever the focus is on the people, the masses, a term as prevalent as it is obscure in her writing.[33] Rosa would not miss a chance to use her unique humour in her writings:

Self-portrait, *c.* 1909. 'To be a human being means to joyfully toss your entire life "on the giant scales of fate" it if must be so, and at the same time to rejoice in the brightness of every day and the beauty of every cloud.'

OH! how – German is this German revolution! How sober, how pedantic, how without buoyancy, without glory, without highness! The forgotten question of capital punishment is only one small individual phase. But how such small matters betray the inner spirit that animates the whole! Liebknecht and I promised our companions in misery – he to his shaven prison mates and I to my poor dear prostitutes and thieves among whom I had spent three and a half years – we promised them, by all that was holy to us, as they looked after us with longing, sorrowful eyes: we will not forget you![34]

Rosa's inimitable position as a well-known political prisoner did not disengage her from others in society. The poor sex workers were as integral to the revolution as Schneiderman.

The revolutionary spirit in her adopted homeland did not leave Rosa untouched. In a piece entitled, lyrically, 'The Acheron in Motion' (November 1918), she wrote, 'Acheron is in motion, and the dwarfs who carry on their little game at the head of the revolution will either tumble head over heels or finally learn to understand the colossal importance of the world historical drama in which they are cast.'[35] The continuation of her emphasis from the 1905 revolution is apparent here. Strikes are the way to transform a revolution from a political to an economic one, for a revolution must always be both. And yet, again, always attentive to both the intricate details and the overarching whole, in the article 'Socialization of Society' (December 1918) Rosa discussed various aspects of the process of making a society socialist: 'Political power, however, is for us socialists only a means. The end for which we must use this power is the fundamental transformation of the entire economic relations.'[36] She was also aware of how the how revolutions could affect women and men differently. In this text she elaborated on socialized child-rearing, care for the elderly and public health, all issues relating intimately to women's lives. Focus on 'the day after' the revolution appeared more and more in her work.

Although the Spartacus League had been a political presence in Germany since 1914, the revolutionary moment allowed it the opportunity to bolster its ranks and promote its message. In 'What Does the Spartacus League Want?' (1918), its goals are forcefully articulated. Luxemburg presented a discussion of the unfolding events and stated that

> The people – betrayed for four years, having forgotten
> culture, honesty, and humanity in the service of the

Moloch, available for every obscene deed – awoke from its four-year long paralysis, only to face the abyss . . . With the conclusion of world war, the class rule of the bourgeoisie has forfeited its right to existence. It is no longer capable of leading society out of the terrible economic collapse which the imperialist orgy has left in its wake.[37]

What did the Spartacus League want? It stood for anti-militarism, anti-imperialism and humanism. It had clearly stated its agenda for international socialism. The Spartacus League demanded the disarmament of police and members of the ruling class; it wanted a militia of the proletariat. Workers' councils were to replace all previous political organs; these were central to the political programme and the ethos of the Spartacus League, and specifically Rosa's own. Moreover, in 'What Does the Spartacus League Want?' Rosa revisited her theory of the general strike as crucial for revolutionary practice. Now she was able to test that theory on her own home ground.

Let us be clear: it is the very essence of this revolution that strikes will become more and more extensive, that they must become more and more the central focus, the key aspect of the revolution. It then becomes an economic revolution, and at the same time a socialist revolution.[38]

The workers' councils were central to Luxemburg's work as well as the battle between socialism and capitalism.[39] Liebknecht's slogan was 'supreme authority for the workers' and soldiers' councils'.[40] The councils were by nature revolutionary institutions and embodied Luxemburg's lifelong admiration for democracy from below. Rosa also saw them as a place in which the education of the masses could take place, allowing for the people's revolutionary consciousness to develop. They were suppressed by the right wing of the SPD, however, showing the final concession in practice to sustaining any socialist ethos it had embodied nationally as well as internationally: 'what is the program of the new government? It proposes the election of a President, who is to have a position intermediate between that of the king of England and that of the president of the United States. He is to be as it were, king Eberts.'[41] Rosa showed that reform of the parliamentary system merely ensured that authority changed from old hands to new – it did not decentralize government or give more power to the masses. While Rosa was marching in Berlin, revolutionary socialism was far from being successful within the masses. She remained an outlier even when the revolution was taking hold in Berlin, proving this was not the revolution for which she agitated.

Christmastime was always much loved by Rosa, and yet that of 1918 was marked by constant commotion. Rosa did not miss the chance to send a letter dated 20 December to her old comrade Lenin, who was facing a completely different set of challenges. She signed it, 'many hand shakes and greetings'.[42] A letter to her dearest Clara stated that 25 December was the first time she was sitting at her own desk after a long spell of travelling. She was well aware of the death threats from a variety of reactionary and counter-revolutionary sources against her, yet never ceased speaking, writing and publishing. At least we can hope that, following her incarceration, she was finally reunited with her beloved Mimi. On 26 December 1918 she refused an offer to visit Clara owing to an overload of work for the *Rote Fahne* newspaper, but wrote that 'my little home is naturally at your disposal and awaits you.'[43] Another later letter states: 'I myself am so much in tumult and turmoil that I have no time to even think about how I am. "C'est la revolution". If only I knew that you were well, then for me everything would go splendidly, A thousand greetings to all of you, sent in haste. I embrace you with all my heart, your RL.'[44]

From her earliest days in the movement until this moment, Rosa always lived happily in the storm.

On 29 December the KPD, German Communist Party, was established, with Rosa Luxemburg as one of its founding members. It was established as a result of the union of International Socialists of Germany (ISD) with the IKD (International Communists), which had largely taken over the local SPD apparatus to unite with the Spartacists.[45] The party included two of Rosa's ex-lovers, both of whom she collaborated with politically, Leo Jogiches and Kostja Zetkin. The party decided, despite Rosa's advice, to boycott the National Assembly elections due in January. On the last day of December 1918, Rosa delivered an impassioned speech, 'Our Program and Political Situation', which exemplified her deep understanding of history and temporality at a time of revolution:

> Our motto is: In the beginning was the act. And the act must be that workers and soldiers councils realize their mission and learn to become the sole public power of the whole nation. Only in this way can we mine the ground so that it will be ready for the revolution which will crown our work.[46]

It was greeted by tumultuous applause.

Late December marked the rise of counter-revolution, and early January marked the resignation of three SPD ministers from the government, while groups of revolutionary workers occupied the editorial offices of Rosa's old haunt, the *Vorwärts*, still the official journal of the SPD. A total of 500,000 workers went on strike and took to the streets to protest. The extreme Right had conducted a full coup against the Spartacists, but alliances were made in an effort to restore the old order. Throughout December an alliance of monarchists and counter-revolutionaries hunted down the Spartacus League. The government-funded Anti-Bolshevik League plastered posters inciting violence:

Workers! Citizens!
The downfall of the Fatherland is imminent!
Save it!
It is not being threatened from without, but from within:
By the Spartacist Group.
Strike its leader dead!
Kill Liebknecht!
You will then have peace, work and bread!
Signed Soldiers from the Front.[47]

Mathilde Jacob recalled hearing excited conversations about her friend Rosa: 'she should be cut to pieces and given to wild beasts'.[48] Rosa was once again on the run, staying at different hotels, always shifting addresses. The streets of Berlin were the sites of clashes between revolutionary and counter-revolutionary forces. Events were fast unfolding. Berlin was in disorder. On 5 January 1919 Berlin USPD leadership, Revolutionary Stewards and the executive of KPD issued a joint statement calling on the masses 'not to accept the attempt of the government to stifle the revolution with bayonets'.[49] Six days later, on 11 January, Rosa wrote to Clara, warning her off visiting too soon, and saw the Spartacist defeats as only a momentary setback. Leo Jogiches and others had been arrested. 'For today I have to close. I embrace you a thousand times, your R.'[50]

On 14 January Rosa Luxemburg wrote 'Order Reigns in Berlin'. A sober, disillusioned text, it was her commentary on the current stage of the revolution: 'The whole path of socialism, as far as revolutionary struggles are concerned, is paved with sheer defeats. And yet, this same history leads step by step, irresistibly, to the ultimate victory!'[51]

The final victory is necessary. The final goal is everything. The price paid on the march towards it was to be extremely high. Rosa argued in 'Order Reigns in Berlin' that the revolutionary struggle is antithetical to parliamentary struggle. She demarcates the contradiction between the movement of the masses on the streets and the indecisive line taken by the leadership. But Rosa was never left without hope and belief in 'the masses':

> The leadership failed. But a new leadership can and must be created by the masses and out of the masses. The masses are the crucial factor. They are the rock on which the ultimate victory of the revolution will be built. The masses were up to the task. They fashioned this 'defeat' into a part of those historical defeats which constitute the pride and power of international socialism. And that is why this 'defeat' is the seed of the future triumph.[52]

Her faith in humanity was unique and unflinching. The masses – human beings, the material of the body politic – are always and exclusively, according to Rosa Luxemburg, their own saviours. They will overcome.

> 'Order reigns in Berlin!' You stupid lackeys! Your 'order' is built on sand. The revolution will 'raise itself up again clashing', and to your horror it will proclaim to the sound of trumpets: *I was, I am, I shall be!*[53]

On the evening of 15 January, five members of the counter-revolutionary Hilmersdorfer Burgerwehr, a reactionary citizens' militia, walked into a bar on the corner of Mannheimer Strasse and Berliner Strasse in Berlin.[54] The five men asked the bartender about a person named Marcusson located next door, in a room where they hoped to find a Spartacist meeting place. Their intent, however, was solely to find a man and a woman. Upon entering the house under the claim of wanting to bring Luxemburg false identification papers, they searched the gentlemen in the room and found a residency permit in Liebknecht's name. The men found a woman who 'appeared suspicious'. That woman was Rosa

Luxemburg. At 9 p.m. a man entered the same house, where Rosa had just been arrested. Wilhelm Pieck, a leading member of KPD, as well as Liebknecht, had been arrested and searched too.

At the same time the Freikorps, battalions of counter-revolutionaries composed mainly of First World War veterans who opposed the republic and had become part of a mercenary private army, had been searching for Karl Liebknecht and Rosa Luxemburg throughout the city. There was surveillance of Liebknecht's correspondence and searches for Luxemburg's whereabouts. No facade of rule of law was given to any of those actions. A phone call to the chancellery's deputy press officer, Robert Breuer, informed those who approved the arrests that without a warrant the arrests were illegal.

Around 9.30 p.m., Liebknecht was brought to Hotel Eden. Pieck and Luxemburg were brought into the hotel by the same men around 10 p.m. Karl Liebknecht was led into a salon, where he still identified himself as Marcusson. By 9.45, naval troops had arrived and around 10.30, Liebknecht was led down the steps of the side exit, insulted and spat at by hotel guests witnessing the events as well as by men in uniform. Former soldier and anti-communist activist Otto Runge struck him with the butt of his rifle. A man punched Liebknecht in the face. They proceeded to murder him; they left his body in a first aid station near Berlin Zoo at 11.15 p.m., where it would remain unidentified.

While her closest comrade Liebknecht was walking towards his death, insults of 'whore' were being thrown at Luxemburg, as she was moved to the first floor of the hotel. Pabst, a far right anti-communist activist, recalled his first encounter with her: 'are you Frau Luxemburg?' he asked. 'Please decide for yourself,' came the response. 'According to the picture it must be you.' To which Rosa replied: 'if you say so!' Encountering Pabst, Rosa sat down to read Goethe's *Faust*, a favourite literary work throughout her life. ('These rhyming lines have been going around in my head since Easter,' she had written in a letter in 1917 about *Faust*.)[55] Rosa was reading while mending the hem of her dress, which had become dishevelled in the process of the arrest.

Vogel, a former soldier who led the arrests, let Rosa Luxemburg walk in front of him through the revolving doors on departing the hotel, whereupon Runge struck her violently with the butt of his rifle. She fell backwards, unconscious, losing a shoe and her handbag in the process. Another counter-revolutionary, Albert Freiherr von Wechmar, stole a letter from her bag written by Clara Zetkin.[56] The woman who always marched onwards, always meticulously put together, in the last moment of consciousness had her dignity stolen from her. It is telling that in Rosa's handbag at a time of great crisis and danger, she carried a letter from her closest female comrade. Runge hit Luxemburg with a second blow while she was on the ground. She was dragged to a car and into the back seat as blood streamed from her nose and mouth. Unconscious, Rosa was delivered another blow from the front seat. The car raced through the cold Berlin night towards the Cornelius Bridge.

A shot fired at close range brought Rosa Luxemburg's life to its untimely end at 23.45 p.m. on 15 January. She drew her very last breath at the Cornelius Bridge, the water of the Landwehrkanal flowing by.

In Goethe's *Faust*, the last book Rosa read before her death, Margareta reflects on her death:[57]

If my grave's out there,
If death is waiting, come with me! No,
From here to my everlasting tomb
And not one step further I'll go![58]

Imprisoned, Margareta, contemplating her march towards death, recites, 'Just follow the path, up the stream, uphill.'

It is hard to imagine the last thoughts going through the ever imaginative, uniquely brilliant mind of Rosa Luxemburg as she was walking towards her death, not far from the Tiergarten, in the same hinterlands in which she adamantly took her daily walk in 1898, when first arriving in Berlin.[59] One may write Rosa's epitaph when reflecting on the dialectic between agency and history: 'You see, I've learnt from the history of the past few years, and looking farther back, from history as a whole, that one should not overestimate the impact or effect that one individual can have.'[60]

On 17 January, Lenin received a laconic telegram from Leo announcing that 'Rosa Luxemburg and Karl Liebknecht had carried out their ultimate revolutionary duty.'[61] Lenin would receive no more 'handshakes in writing', as she had written to him in the past, from Dr Luxemburg. Despite their disagreements and her misreadings of the new realities of the Russian Revolution, these two leaders – who worked ceaselessly to create a new world – were bound together in uniquely revolutionary times.

Rosa was granted her last revolutionary wish, however. A woman whose life was intertwined with the revolution, as a concept, ethos and reality, had always dreamt of dying on the march. The sharp divide between public reactions – shifting between intense reverence and hatred towards a mutilated body swimming in the Landwehrkanal, and deep mourning for a friend and ally – are a lesson to all of Rosa Luxemburg's future readers and those inspired by her. Her extraordinary life leaves us much to reflect upon, particularly the biggest lessons we all face in our own lives: how to pass on a better world to those that follow. Rosa's murder occurred during the height of the stormy revolutionary moment, and her legacy continues to draw heated critique and passionate debate. Despite mistakes, losses and failures, Rosa Luxemburg never wavered from her revolutionary cause. Her words, her deeds, her loves and losses marched on. In the last letter known to have been penned by Rosa, on 11 January 1919, addressed to Clara Zetkin, Rosa wrote: 'one has to take history as it comes, whatever course it takes.'[62]

6

Discord Marching On

In a memorial speech in honour of Rosa Luxemburg, Paul Levi said: 'the revolution proceeds along its road, a road marked out with milestones, and these milestones are hills of corpses.'[1] On 13 June 1919, a quiet procession, acting as a peaceful protest, joined Rosa's physical body as it was finally interred in her resting place. Rosa's friends and relatives walked with her during her earthly body's final movements; Rosa's brother and nephew were in the procession. (Her family had retained contact with her, when her turbulent life allowed it – often it was dangerous to be close to Rosa.)

A few lines written in her text on Korolenko provide an ironic commentary to the events of 15 January 1919: 'these executions were exceptional, but they left a deep impression upon the people.'[2] Zetkin wrote later, in 1921, in the newspaper *Workers' Dreadnought*, edited by Rosa's comrade sister Sylvia Pankhurst: 'Rosa Luxemburg was a woman of indomitable will. Severe self control put a curb on the mettlesome ardour of her temperament, veiling it with an outwardly reserved and calm demeanor.'[3] The changes within German society were swift; they soon became a fully blown descent into fascism. The Friekorps, the voluntary extra-parliamentary organization that had played a part in Rosa's untimely death, became the fertile ground for the development of National Socialism. The leaders of the Freikorps retreated to Bavaria, where they came under the influence of the rising political agitator Adolf Hitler.[4]

On 30 August 1932, 75-year-old Clara Zetkin climbed the stairs of the Reichstag, as its oldest member, to open what would be its last session. Clara's steps were slow and she was leaning on her comrades. Clara was nearly blind, incredibly frail and unwell; her steps were a world away from the youthful ones alongside her friend and comrade Rosa Luxemburg. Clara went on to deliver a 45-minute speech against fascism, in which she expressed how the attack on labour laws and collective action had led to the current fascist government. She warned against lax responses towards the rise in hatred and division. 'The battle must be fought particularly in order to defeat fascism, which intends to destroy with blood and iron all clear expressions of the workers.'[5] She continued: 'The masses must not allow themselves to be frightened by the brutal use of force by which capitalism seeks its survival in the form of new world wars and fascist civil strife.'[6] Nevertheless, the effect of Nazism on Rosa's closest circle was immediate.

In 1933 the Nazis had the red star removed from the monument erected near the graves of Luxemburg and Liebknecht. Her books were among those burnt by Joseph Goebbels on 10 May 1933.[7] Within German fascism, the rise in attacks on communists and Jews made her closest comrades vulnerable. Clara died in June 1933 in exile. Mathilde Jacob, Rosa's beloved right hand, who was responsible for the preservation and publication of much of Rosa's work, was taken away on 27 July 1942 and deported to the Theresienstadt concentration camp, where she died on 14 April 1943. She humbly noted, 'I march as a simple soldier in the Spartacus league, but I never lost courage for the fight.'[8] Like so many, she was not significant enough in the socialist ranks to be hunted by Hitler and the Nazis for her politics, but she suffered for her Jewishness, like all of her and Rosa's brethren in the 1930s. Luise Kautsky died in Auschwitz at the age of eighty from a heart attack.

A nearly blind Clara Zetkin leaving the opening of the Reichstag in 1932, as its oldest member. She spoke about the connection between economic oppression and fascism: 'I am opening this Congress in the fulfilment of my duties as honorary president and in the hope that despite my current infirmities, I may yet have the fortune to open as honorary president of the first Soviet Congress of a Soviet Germany.'

But the story of that portion of my life's path which I walked jointly with Rosa – I should almost like to any, hand in hand with her –, seemed to me to be of interest to a wider circle, and at the same time its publication meant the fulfillment in a certain degree of the terms of a legacy and the squaring of an old account of gratitude. For my whole being, yes, the whole content of my life has been immensely enriched by my connection and friendship with Rosa Luxemburg.[9]

Mathilde Jacob recounted: 'Yes, it was always profitable to walk with Rosa Luxemburg. It was part of her nature to make her rich knowledge accessible to others.'[10]

Levi proceeded to take on the position as the head of the KPD, which had conceded its democratic impulse.[11] The KPD had mythologized Rosa and its anti-democratic tendencies led to an ideological misreading of her archive against her intentions. In 1922 Clara Zetkin had argued that Luxemburg had begun to revise her views in the last months of her life, and was well on the road to Leninism at the time of her assassination.[12] And yet it has been shown that a consistent democratic thread in Luxemburg's work refutes Zetkin's argument. The discussion around debates between Lenin and Luxemburg remains vivid and fraught, mostly because of the conflation of Lenininsm and Luxemburgism with the actual writings of these two radicals.

A challenge to Luxemburg's position on the Polish question has come in the twenty-first century from Eric Blanc, who reopened archives of the PPS, Rosa's first nemesis upon entering the stage of world politics.[13] The archives showed her position towards PPS came from a realpolitik incentive rather than a comprehensive political and ethical agenda, her incipient critiques of reformism as well as her emphasis on spontaneity. An overarching concern of Blanc's work is the 'myth' of Luxemburg the humanist – he questions the analysis which portrays her as a flawless thinker and activist with significance in twenty-first-century politics and activism. Blanc's revelations are substantial and informative. It is without doubt that Luxemburg did not always practice what she preached; and within her 'own' party she displayed centralist tendencies – advocating policies she believed were right, rather than asking for popular support – which stood in sharp contrast to her ethos of insisting on democratic tendencies with Marxism. Yet the archive as it has been presented here speaks for itself; Luxemburg's democratic insistence runs as a red thread throughout her life's work, alongside her revolutionary impetus. Her legacy lived on outside of scholarly debates within the realm of German communism.

In 1951 a monument bearing the words 'the dead are a constant reminder' was erected next to the graves of Luxemburg and Liebknecht. Every year on 15 January, the GDR commemorated Luxemburg and Liebknecht, who were seen as their martyrs. But Luxemburg's spectre relentlessly haunted any and all sources of authority. In 1988, shortly before the fall of the Berlin Wall, in Rosa's adopted home, political dissenters unrolled a banner carrying Rosa's famous quip: 'Freedom is always the freedom of those who think differently.' They were immediately arrested, but the testimony to Luxemburg's defence of democracy within dictatorship from the Left had once again lived on.[14]

The legacy of Rosa Luxemburg took the contradictions and complications of her life beyond any imagined horizon. Celebrated historian Jörn Schütrumpf, Head of Research at the Rosa-Luxemburg-Stiftung, identifies Luxemburg's legacy with freedom and emancipation of the individual as well as society as a whole, and as an exemplar of unity of theory and action.[15] He sees her legacy as epitomized around honesty towards one's own actions, genuine thought and decency in her relationships.[16] The English Trotskyist activist Tony Cliff claimed no less than two different mottos used by Rosa Luxemburg ('doubt all' epigraph and 'at the beginning was the deed' as her 'motto') and suggests a third possible one, 'do not cry, do not laugh, but understand', all quotations from Luxemburg though none claimed by herself as her motto.[17] Rosa certainly never identified with the seventeenth-century philosopher Spinoza. Rather, her motto, taken from one of her letters, was 'here I stand, I can do no other.' She never stood still, and never easily agreed to others' definitions of her being, in her life or afterlife.

Alongside the appreciation of Rosa Luxemburg's political and economic work, the publication of her letters from the 1920s onward created a rift in her reception that contributed to such debates as the above. The creation of the image of a romantic, bird-loving woman, living with depression, began to emerge. Elzbieta Ettinger's biography of 1979 developed this image (the book includes little or no discussion of Luxemburg's work), as do various works that draw exclusively on her letters. Margarethe von Trotta's film *Rosa Luxemburg* (1986) visualized a lonely, depressed woman. Rosa Luxemburg was a complex and often contradictory personality, and no doubt suffered lows as well as highs; yet it was her multidimensionality as well as her resilience which sustained her throughout an immensely turbulent life. The letters show not only a constant thread of care for the world around her and commitment to the cause, but a sincere joy in her own work and pride in what she knew was her unique intellectual brilliance. Whether she was right or wrong on specific questions, it is without doubt that her intellectual contribution to the Marxist canon is beyond measure. Reading either parts of Luxemburg's life – the letters or the scholarly work – inevitably will give a very partial image of an inimitable activist and writer.

It is no easy task to write about Luxemburg's psyche and personal relationships. She kept her emotional affairs distinct from her public persona, and her letters quite clearly were not intended for publication. Many archival materials are still being unearthed and recovered. There are two major biographies of Luxemburg available in English; the first, published by her comrade Paul Frolich in 1939, brings much information and personal perspective (Frolich was the partner of Rosa's beloved student Rosi Wolfstein). However, its strength is also its weakness; the work often treats Luxemburg as friend rather than subject. A second biography was published by J. P. Nettl in 1966 in two volumes, then in 1969 in an abridged format. It was republished in 2019. This is an extensive study of not only Luxemburg's life, but the times she lived in, and it includes vast political and historical context crucial for understanding her work. Recently, significant work has been carried out by Rory Castle Jones, who has unearthed new archival materials, and has specialized in examining Rosa's early years in light of these discoveries. Indeed, my own work has benefited hugely from Castle Jones's research, especially his refutation of the myths haunting her archive with regard to her Jewishness and relationship to her gender.

Georg Lukács argued that despite the fact that Rosa's solution to the problem raised in *The Accumulation of Capital* was false, her focus – on the problem of imperialism within capitalism – was significant.[18]

More than a century after its publication, Luxemburg's most famous text, *The Accumulation of Capital*, still elicits debates and responses. Some of the major questions that arise – some answered, some left open – remain timely and necessary within theoretical and political debates of the twenty-first century. Specifically, attempts to claim Luxemburg was anti-racist or anti-colonialist are never completely successful, owing to their anachronistic definitions for contemporary readers. The complexity of *Accumulation* and *Anti-critique* means that there are rich resources within the text, but never unequivocal answers. The attention to history that motivated Rosa Luxemburg's work means that transporting her directly to our time is a futile task. Still, the theoretical legacy she left has opened up multiple debates and answered many urgent questions of our times.

The philosopher Michael Brie notes that the crises arising from neoliberal financial market capitalism brought a return to the *Accumulation*, since it posited a theoretical question about the limits of expansion for capitalist markets.[19] A central debate looks at the implications of this text for current ideas around post-colonialism and anti-imperialism. Some commentators link this critique with other texts in which Luxemburg shows overwhelming interest in – and compassion towards – non-Western societies that are non-capitalist economies. While highlighting the much-needed emphasis on Luxemburg's racist tones – she assumed the non-capitalist and non-Western world would be part of the world revolution, but not of its own agency, rather it would be acted upon by the Western proletariat – Kanishka Chowdhury revisits Luxemburg's argument that political violence is a vehicle for economic process and that both are bound up with each other through the very conditions of the reproduction of capital.[20] General Editor of the *Complete Works of Rosa Luxemburg* Peter Hudis argues that 'Luxemburg's detailed investigation of the indigenous communal social formations of Asian, African and Latin American societies, both before and after the intrusion of European imperialism, represent one of the most systematic discussions of their significance ever penned in the Marxist tradition.'[21] Hudis notes: 'As I have detailed elsewhere, this distinguished Luxemburg's position from that of Marx, who did not share the unilinear evolutionist assumption that pre-capitalist communal formations were "anywhere and everywhere" "doomed to destruction" upon contact with capitalism.'[22] At the same time, Hudis acknowledges the same limitation argued by Chowdhury, according to which Rosa did not see the inhabitants of the colonized world as agents of progress themselves.[23] Luxemburg, following her comrades of the Second International, saw history as following a linear path. Another perspective is provided by Helen Scott, who shows that opening our own historical perspective to a multilinear and multifaceted understanding of capitalism and history allows for new possibilities in rethinking the relationship between Luxemburg and post-colonialism. Scott argues that 'Luxemburg positioned imperialism as not only the property of "the West", but of capitalism. Second, she articulated a strategy for emancipation grounded in international working-class solidarity wherein struggles for liberation and against oppression are inseparable from labour struggles and vice versa.'[24] For Rosa, countering oppression was an enterprise for both heart and mind, and her analysis was focused on expanding her humanism towards societies and people she had never physically encountered.

One of the most significant aspects of the *Accumulation*'s legacy is the relevance of its argument for a feminist critique of capitalism. 'The Woman Question' continues to haunt us as much as it did in Rosa's own lifetime. Ankica Čakardić responded to Luxemburg in her own domain: Marxian economics and political theory. Starting with a focus on Luxemburg's critique of bourgeois feminism, which has been illuminated in this work, Čakardić argues that whereas Luxemburg was not an organizer and thus did not concern herself much with the organization of working women, she 'fervently supported the organisational work of the socialist women's movement, understanding the importance and difficulties of work-life for female emancipation'.[25] For Luxemburg the question of women's suffrage was tactical, as it formalized an already established 'political maturity' of proletarian women. This is not a question of supporting an isolated case of suffrage, but support for universal suffrage, 'through which the women's socialist movement can further develop a strategy for the struggle for emancipation of women and the working class in general'.[26] Čakardić then moves to make a shift inspired by Luxemburg in style and content both – focusing not only on her own context, but on feminist debates within the Left at the moment. She provides a radical re-reading of the *Accumulation* that utilizes its argument to reflect upon the exploitation of labour in the household – a non-capitalist realm, but a sphere of labour. These readings use Luxemburg's argument to claim that capitalism requires a non-capitalist sphere – namely, the household – in order to expand in its demand. Utilizing the spatial argument about interdependent dynamics between capitalism and non-capitalist economy, Čakardić extends the basic structural argument of *The Accumulation of Capital*: capitalism needs a non-capitalist sphere into which it can expand. Čakardić argues:

> According to Luxemburg's economic theory, the capitalist mode of production reproduces itself by creating surplus-values, the

appropriation of which can only be hastened by a concomitant expansion in surplus-creating capitalist production. Hence, it is necessary to ensure that production is reproduced in a larger volume than before, meaning that the expansion of capital is the absolute law governing the survival of any individual capitalist. In *The Accumulation of Capital* Rosa Luxemburg establishes the premises for understanding capitalism as a social relation which permanently produces crises and necessarily faces objective limits to demand and self-expansion. In this sense she developed a theory of imperialism based on an analysis of the process of social production and accumulation of capital realised via various 'non-capitalist formations', in this case, the household.[27]

This reading aligns the critique with contemporary Marxist feminists such as Silvia Federici and campaigns such as Wages for Housework.

A significant study of Luxemburg's life and thought is Raya Dunayevskaya's *Rosa Luxemburg, Women's Liberation, and Marx's Philosophy of Revolution* (1982). Dunayevskaya was the American founder of the philosophy of Marxist humanism in the United States. The first to translate Marx's economic and philosophic manuscripts, she was kicked down the stairs for suggesting to young communists they should actually read some Trotksy before they decide they disagreed with him. She herself worked with Trotsky as a secretary until she broke with him theoretically. Dunayevskaya's study is a critical intellectual biography highlighting Luxemburg's inseparability of theory and action. A significant intervention of her study is that she claims Luxemburg as a feminist in theory and practice. The book's argument is complex and essential, tracing Luxemburg's importance for the women's liberation movement at Dunayevskaya's own time of writing in the early 1980s, as well as highlighting sexism in Luxemburg's life and how that translates to the present moment. Her reading of politics from below – fomented through organization and education, both considered crucial for the anti-racist and women's liberation movements of Dunayevskaya's time – is deeply grounded in Luxemburg's work. 'Luxemburg's generalizations are relevant for our day and we must examine them. There is absolutely no doubt that not only is there a need for a great deal more democracy, for different tendencies to express themselves, but even for a totally new concept of democracy, like Luxemburg's.'[28] Most profoundly, she applies lessons of both Luxemburg's life and work to women's liberation, from an emphasis on her friendship with Clara Zetkin to the end of her romantic relationship with Jogiches – arguing against the 'typical male attitude' that claims that Rosa's most intellectual period occurred after the break-up.[29] At the same time it is vital to consider the statement below:

> Time is now to be considered as Marx defined it: 'Time is space for human development'. Rooted in such a concept, we want to take a look at Luxemburg as original character, as revolutionary theorist, and as a feminist; although she might sometimes appear as a reluctant feminist, she is always a revolutionary.[30]

To regard Luxemburg as a role model and apply her theory beyond its literal sphere of application is a hugely significant move; no doubt Dunayevskaya, a revolutionary woman, an outsider, in her own right, was perfectly placed to pick up those threads of Rosa's life.

Rosa Luxemburg's radical legacy has inspired and galvanized into action many women. Barbara Hahn, in her *The Jewess Pallas Athena: This Too a Theory of Modernity* (2005), wrote the chapter 'Kaddish for RL', in which she elaborates on the two sides of Rosa: unwavering politician and sentimental woman.[31] As this book has argued, Rosa was both. Hahn discusses Rosa's similarities and differences to Rahel Varnhagen, and connects her to another interlocutor from the future, Hannah Arendt. For Hahn, Jewishness was inescapable for Rosa, and sexism was something that she had to live with and her legacy has had to combat.[32] Strikingly, many writings on Luxemburg feature discussion of the complexities of her relationship with Jogiches, her physical appearance and her sentimental personality features, without pausing to reflect on the fact that no male author would ever receive such a treatment. Rosa never wanted to be mythicized, yet she was: for some, she was a romantic lover of nature; for others, an unwaveringly ruthless revolutionary. Rosa was neither and both. Human beings are complex, and rarely meet each other's expectations.

Hannah Arendt reviewed Nettl's biography in the *New York Review of Books* in 1966, and Arendt's essay on Luxemburg became one of the selections in her *Men in Dark Times* (1968). The essay pursues a problematic argument. Arendt, herself far from being a careful reader of Marx throughout her life, claimed that Luxemburg 'was not an orthodox Marxist, so little orthodox indeed that it might be doubted that she was a Marxist at all'.[33] This claim of course holds no water. Yet Arendt's review of Luxemburg is twofold, most significantly in the context of Arendt's own life. Arendt's discussion of the significance of the 'peer group' – the Polish friendship group from which Rosa's organization stemmed – is telling. So is her analysis of Luxemburg's relationship with Jogiches, as she explains: 'in marriage, it is not always easy to tell the partners' thoughts apart.'[34] This sentence might as well be applied directly to Arendt's Spartacist husband Heinrich Blücher, to whom she dedicated her *Origins of Totalitarianism*, in which Arendt presents a wide-reaching critique of Stalinist Russia (one of the spheres of thought in which she sees Luxemburg as undoubtedly vindicated is her understanding of the Russian Revolution). Arendt herself was fascinated by the political power of revolution, and shared Luxemburg's belief in the strength of revolutions being built from the ground, among the masses, the people acting in concert with each other. Arendt wrote about Luxemburg as a pariah, 'self-consciously a woman' – two positions that may be applied to herself; she notes the centrality of Rosa's Jewish background and the problematic relationship between cosmopolitanism and Jewishness in *fin de siècle* Europe. Luxemburg was one of the only women to be included in Arendt's intellectual history courses; as she concludes her review, 'one would like to hope that she will finally find her place in the education of political scientists in the countries of the West, for Mr Nettl is right: "her ideas belong wherever the history of political ideas is seriously taught".'

Perhaps ironically, a common thread Luxemburg and Arendt shared was their ideas being used against them. Arendt critiques in the review of Nettl's work the concept of 'Luxemburgism'. Arendt's own archives show a careful consideration of Luxemburg's work. Her personal library contains Luxemburg's writings from 1915 to 1918; and her Library of Congress archives contain meticulous notes collected before she wrote her essay on Luxemburg, including a summary of *The Accumulation of Capital* and a list of its multiple editions, as well as a list of complete works published in English to date. Arendt was certainly not a Marxist, yet understood the weight of addressing a person's work rather than their image or myth. Arendt was herself considered a subversive Jewess; she was referred to as 'the Rosa Luxemburg of nothingness' when writing about the Eichmann trial.[35] Arendt was utilized against her will to defend various positions with which she had nothing in common; a burden with which Luxemburg undoubtedly would have sympathized. The most telling connection between the two women, and one reason for the lifelong admiration of Arendt towards Luxemburg, is the price paid for being a rebellious Jewish woman challenging Jewish nationalism. Arendt never felt fully part of the American world which became her refuge after fleeing the Second World War; thus she shared with Luxemburg the emotional position of being, throughout her life, an outsider, a 'pariah', as Arendt noted in another essay, 'The Jew as Pariah'.

Luxemburg and Arendt are often considered side by side in reflections of dissenting women. Simone Frieling's *Rebellinnen* brings together the legacy of Luxemburg, Arendt and Simone Weil, showing their respective determination and conviction for their respective causes.[36] Crucially for English-speaking readers, Jacqueline Rose's influential re-examination of Luxemburg's legacy in her *Women in Dark Times* (2014) exposed to readers (readers who would not usually pick up a Marxist analysis book) the multidimensionality of Rosa Luxemburg both as a revolutionary woman and a revolutionary thinker. Her re-examination of Luxemburg's life and work in the context of the feminist questions posed in our time reintroduced to audiences the possibilities and imaginaries that this unique woman captured. Rose's reclaiming of Luxemburg for twenty-first-century thinking allows her to develop new conversations and inspire new dialogues, much in the legacy of Luxemburg herself.

Luxemburg's writings regarding activism and anti-colonialism gained her a place in theories of liberation and numerous activist struggles. Ruth First, the celebrated anti-apartheid activist and stalwart of the African National Congress (ANC), writing of the 'Boer War and Union', commented: 'At the same time it must be said that if Olive Schreiner failed on the Boer war, who did not? Perhaps only Rosa Luxemburg.' According to First, it was by analysing 'the historical conditions of capitalist accumulation and the tendency for capital to overwhelm pre-capitalist methods of production' that Rosa Luxemburg was able to have 'illuminated this process through the example of the Boer War'. Rosa's legacy inspired many brave women to follow in her revolutionary footsteps.[37] First famously spent and chronicled 117 days in detention; and, like Luxemburg, First came to a tragic, untimely end. First, like Luxemburg, continues to inspire.

The Rosa-Luxemburg-Stiftung, a global organization, is one of six major foundations in the Federal Republic of Germany aiming to expand political education at home and abroad. Since its founding in 1990, the Stiftung has adhered to the legacy of its namesake and seeks to represent democratic socialism with an unwavering internationalist focus. The Stiftung is committed to a radical perspective emphasizing public awareness, enlightenment and social critique. It stands in the tradition of the workers' and women's movements, as well as anti-fascism and anti-racism.

Rosa Luxemburg's spirit persists in continuing struggles; she is read in languages she never knew, and from China to South America continues to inspire revolutionary work across the world. The Israeli human rights luminary Shulamit Aloni wrote the introduction to the Hebrew edition of Luxemburg's letters from prison. Aloni, also born in Poland, was one of the foremost defenders of Palestinian rights. More recently, Dov Khenin, member of Knesset for the Joint List (representing Palestinian Israelis for which he was the only Jewish MK), foremost environmental activist and central force behind the Israeli Communist Party, published a co-authored collection of essays with Dani Filc, *What Is to Be Done Now*, which draws extensively on Luxemburg's work to address burning issues in Israeli and Palestinian society.[38]

Across the border in Ramallah, 'freedom is always the freedom of dissenters' is inscribed upon a building. Rosa's lifelong passion for culture and literature lives on in her reception as well. Luxemburg opposed Jewish nationalism as well as other forms of nationalism, and thus is an invaluable resource for those resisting nationalistic motivated expansion, colonialism, of all kinds around the world. Paul Le Blanc revisits Rosa's anti-colonialism in the context of world literature, placing her opposite Herman Melville, Joseph Conrad, Mark Twain, Rudyard Kipling and George Orwell. Dark horrors are visited upon innumerable victims in Africa, Asia, Latin America, and among indigenous peoples of Australia and North America – what Luxemburg referred to as 'the unspoiled remainder of the noncapitalist world environment.' Le Blanc forcefully argues for the power of her work:

A work of art twists reality in order to squeeze out truths not otherwise seen. The same is true of theory. Some things are emphasised, others minimised, connections between cause and effect are established . . . Things that are marginalised can end up having central importance. The truth emphasised by the work of art or the theoretical construct may continue to have validity – but multiple theorisations may highlight the complexities.[39]

Luxemburg's critique of capitalism's tendency to violate unspoiled nature leads to an understanding of the force of art in critiquing capitalist expansionism. Luxemburg scholar Helen Scott's work on both the reception of Luxemburg as well as her own focus on literature is crucial for understanding Rosa and her legacy. Culture was central to the Luxemburg home, and Rosa found great joy in music and literature throughout her life. Scott connects the many literary references in letters and formal writings to 'Luxemburg's sharp awareness of the capacity of literature to engage the senses and impact us emotionally in ways that bypass intellectual processes'.[40] Luxemburg's own literary analysis

held together complex and contradictory forces: she both traces the complex relationships between historical and cultural developments, unearthing the class roots of literature, *and* insists that each work is more than simply the sum of its socio-historical parts, and must be appreciated on its own terms, according to the particular elements of genre and form.[41]

Beyond Luxemburg being 'an original personality', she appreciated the interlinking between form, content and reception. Culture should not be didactic, yet can reveal injustices in society as well as possible horizons in which those injustices might cease to exist.

Rosa Luxemburg's murder, in its turn, catalysed some literary and cultural responses. Karl Kraus, satirist and writer, used to travel in Germany and read aloud Rosa's famous buffalo letter, to which he received an angry response from a schoolteacher in 1920 commenting on the false humanism and sentimentality attributed by Luxemburg in the letter to the buffalo. Kraus in turn argued that the human race blames the animal kingdom for its own flaws, and scolded the schoolteacher for her lack of empathy. He published the exchange in the journal *Die Peckel* under the title 'a response to Rosa Luxemburg from an unsentimental woman'. Poetic responses to the woman who knew Goethe and Adam Mickiewicz by heart commemorate her legacy appropriately. Paul Celan wrote of her:

> The man became a sieve, the woman
> Had to swim, the sow,
> For herself, for no-one, for everyone –
> The Landwehrkanal will not root
> Nothing falters.

Bertold Brecht wrote that 'red Rosa has now disappeared', and composed her epitaph, in which he wrote:

> Here lies, buried
> Rosa Luxemburg
> A Jewess from Poland,
> A pioneer of the German working class
> Killed on the orders of
> The German oppressors. You, the oppressed ones,
> Bury your discord.

David Bowie was inspired to write his song 'The Drowned Girl' (1982) by Brecht's poem of a similar title, originally called 'On the Girl Beaten to Death', also in memory of Rosa. Bowie's voice strangely and vividly expresses the act and feelings of drowning.

'Red Rosa' leaves prison. Illustration by Kate Evans.

No one had witnessed Rosa's death, yet her commemoration in culture has kept her spirit alive. More recently Rosa received a special tribute in an art form close to her heart. A talented, self-trained artist, whose drawings and paintings occupy many of her letters, Rosa became the subject of a graphic novel, *Red Rosa*. Kate Evans vividly brought Rosa to life by drawing on countless archival sources, specialist materials, expositions of Rosa's materials and the historical context of her time, all presented in a singular graphic narrative. Evans's work is extraordinary in form and content, evoking the spirit of Rosa Luxemburg, who wrote about her constant quest for innovation: 'it is the form that no longer satisfies me.'

The memorial on the Landwehrkanal, the site of Rosa Luxemburg's murder, photographed exactly a hundred years after the event, on 15 January 2019. Spontaneous tributes of flowers flow throughout the year but especially on this anniversary.

'I didn't want to write until I could report something definite,' wrote Rosa in one of her letters.[42] She provides us with some impetus to think of the march of her legacy onwards: 'Human beings are able to endure much more as individuals, on their own, than as "heroes" to whom the masses look out of slavish obedience.'[43] This work is drawing to a close, and begs to retain the persistence that Rosa Luxemburg's spirit encapsulated, as well as her unique imagination and open-mindedness. This book is written exactly a century after Rosa Luxemburg was murdered. Her death would give way to one of the most vicious and ruthless regimes in history. At the time of writing, the dark days that followed her departure from the world stage are resurfacing and returning to our headlines. Racist and neo-imperalist movements are taking hold of the streets and parliaments around the world. War-mongering leaders make gains on the backs of the poor.

Banner at a commemorative march in memory of Karl Liebknecht and Rosa Luxemburg, 13 January 2019. Tens of thousands joined the march in 2019, which ends traditionally at the memorial to the socialist dead at the Zentralfriedhof Friedrichsfelde, Berlin.

Millions of displaced people are seeking a place they can call home, troubling the borders of our lives. At the same time, the energy, resilience and humanism of Rosa Luxemburg are re-emerging as a counter-force. Millions of people are working to bring down dictators, in solidarity with the poor and displaced, working together for peace and dignity of all humankind. From South Africa to Mexico, from New York to Baghdad, from Gaza to Warsaw, popular resistance and new Rosa Luxemburgs are refusing to accept violence and cruelty as a given and are working towards a better future for the human race. Rosa had her dark moments and her crisis of faith and yet her unwavering humanity and lust for life are a legacy that shines through the years that have passed since she took her last steps on this earth.

Exactly a hundred years after the murder of Rosa Luxemburg thousands of people marched in Berlin in her memory against fascism, capitalism, imperialism and sexism. The divides against which Rosa Luxemburg spent her life fighting had been put aside. Lenininsts and liberal feminists were all singing songs and holding flowers for Red Rosa. She is remembered at times contrary to the humanism that was the central axis of her legacy, yet the extraordinary force of her personality marches on beyond her politics. It is her life's work which resonates a centenary after she took her last steps; the idea of unequivocal commitment for social justice for all is returning to our streets. The shadow of the little great woman is marching on, arguing for freedom from oppression and equality in dignity for all.

The air is cold and crisp in January in Berlin. The trees are bare. There is no birdsong to be heard anywhere. The revolutionary heritage of Rosa Luxemburg continues. Luxemburg was singular in more than one way. Her life was a product of a specific historical contingency and uniquely revolutionary times. Yet, this book is written as a galvanizing intervention for those still working towards a better world for all. The birds are always present, lurking as potential, as is the spirit of the revolution. Whether her ideas were right or wrong, Rosa Luxemburg's bravery, resilience, empathy and ability to see the beauty in the world, even in her darkest moments, inspire us today as we face old challenges anew. Rosa Luxemburg's fierce intellect and stormy heart have left us a calling to answer.

The water of the Landwehrkanal continues to flow alongside the march of history. We have not yet fulfilled our ultimate revolutionary duty to Rosa Luxemburg. The oppressions and injustices against which she fought are still rife. And yet the arc of history, which was galvanized by the determined ideas and heartfelt solidarity of Rosa Luxemburg, continues. She was, she is, she will be. History will do its work. See that you join Rosa Luxemburg's march.

References

Introduction

1 Tony Cliff, Introduction, in Paul Frolich, *Rosa Luxemburg: Ideas in Action* (London 1994), p. ix.

2 Mathilde Jacob, *Rosa Luxemburg: An Intimate Portrait* (London, 2000), p. 13. Luxemburg repeats the same maxim in a letter to Leo Jogiches from 1897, in *The Letters of Rosa Luxemburg*, ed. Georg Adler, Peter Hudis and Annelies Laschitza, trans. George Shriver (London, 2013), p. 32.

3 Drawing here on Arendt's terminology in her famous essay 'The Jew as Pariah', in *The Jewish Writings*, ed. Jerome Kohn and Ron H. Feldman (New York, 2007), pp. 275–98.

4 Letter to Nadina and Boris Krichevsky, in *The Letters of Rosa Luxemburg*, p. 1.

5 Rosa Luxemburg, 'The Spirit of Russian Literature: Life of Korolenko', in *Rosa Luxemburg Speaks*, ed. Mary-Alice Waters (New York, 1970), p. 343.

6 Luxemburg, 'Life of Korolenko', p. 344.

7 Ibid.

8 Rosa Luxemburg, Letter to Kostja Zetkin (1908), in *The Letters of Rosa Luxemburg*, p. 255.

9 Jacob, *An Intimate Portrait*, p. 97.

10 Luxemburg, Letter to Robert Seidel (1898), in *The Letters of Rosa Luxemburg*, p. 65.

1 A Clap of Thunder

1 Paul Frolich, *Rosa Luxemburg: Ideas in Action* (London, 1994), p. 21.

2 Annelies Laschitza, *Rosa Luxemburg. Im Lebensrausch, trotz alledem: Eine Biographie* (Berlin, 2000, Kindle edn), p. 16.

3 Frolich, *Ideas in Action*, p. 22.

4 Rosa Luxemburg, Letter to Sophie Liebknecht (1917), in *The Letters of Rosa Luxemburg*, ed. Georg Adler, Peter Hudis and Annelies Laschitza, trans. George Shriver (London, 2013), p. 412.

5 Rosa Luxemburg, 'The Spirit of Russian Literature: Life of Korolenko', in *Rosa Luxemburg Speaks*, ed. Mary-Alice Waters (New York, 1970), p. 341.

6 Ibid.

7 Laschitza, *Rosa Luxemburg*, p. 19.

8 I follow Kate Evans here in assuming the condition was indeed congenital hip dislocation, formed when a child is born with an unstable hip. This means that the ball will slip out of the socket with movement. The joint may sometimes completely dislocate.

9 J. P. Nettl, *Rosa Luxemburg* (London, 1966), p. 35.

10 Ibid., p. 56.

11 Frolich, *Ideas in Action*, p. 25.

12 Nettl, *Rosa Luxemburg*, p. 56.

13 Luxemburg, Letter to Luise Kautsky (1904), in *The Letters of Rosa Luxemburg*, p. 177.

14 Jörn Schütrumpf, *Rosa Luxemburg; or, The Price of Freedom* (Berlin, 2008), p. 12.

15 Laschitza, *Rosa Luxemburg*, p. 30.

16 Frolich, *Ideas in Action*, p. 36.

17 Ibid., p. 57.

18 Rosa Luxemburg, 'In Memory of the Proletarian Party', available online at www.marxists.org., accessed 3 February 2019.

19 Ibid.

20 Nettl, *Rosa Luxemburg*, p. 59.

21 Long after Rosa Luxemburg's departure from the earth, James Joyce lived on Universitätstrasse too.

22 Frolich, *Ideas in Action*, p. 30.

23 Nettl, *Rosa Luxemburg*, p. 64.

24 Katharina Rowold, *The Educated Woman: Minds, Bodies, and Women's Higher Education in Britain, Germany, and Spain, 1865–1914* (Oxford, 2012), p. 69.

25 Schütrumpf, *The Price of Freedom*, p. 14.

26 Frolich, *Ideas in Action*, p. 31.

27 Laschitza, *Rosa Luxemburg*, p. 66.

28 Rosa Luxemburg, 'The Industrial Development of Poland', in *The Complete Works of Rosa Luxemburg*, vol. 1: *Economic Writings 1*, ed. Peter Hudis (London, 2014), p. 43.

29 Frolich, *Ideas in Action*, p. 41.

30 For an elaboration of this issue in Luxemburg's work, see Michal Kasprzak, 'Dancing with the Devil: Rosa Luxemburg's Conception of the Nationality Question in Polish Socialism', *Critique*, XL/3 (2012), pp. 423–48.

31 Luxemburg, 'Industrial Development of Poland', p. 74.

32 Peter Hudis, Introduction, in Luxemburg, *Complete Works*, vol. 1.

33 Luxemburg, Letter to Leo Jogiches (March 1894), in *The Letters of Rosa Luxemburg*, p. 12.

34 Luxemburg, Letter to Leo Jogiches (1894), in *Comrade and Lover: Letters to Leo Jogiches*, ed. Elzbieta Ettinger (Cambridge, MA, 1979), p. 64.

35 Luxemburg, Letter to Leo Jogiches (July 1897), ibid., p. 35.

36 Luxemburg, Letter to Leo Jogiches (June 1898), ibid., p. 80.

37 Luxemburg, Letter to Leo Jogiches (1897), ibid., p. 87.

38 Luxemburg, Letter to Leo Jogiches (July 1897), ibid., p. 35.

39 Luxemburg, Letter to Leo Jogiches (March 1894), ibid., p. 8.

40 Luxemburg, Letter to Leo Jogiches (1899), in *Comrade and Lover: Letters to Leo Jogiches*, p. 76.

41 Luxemburg, Letter to Leo Jogiches (May 1894), in *The Letters of Rosa Luxemburg*, p. 42.

42 Rosa Luxemburg, 'The Dreyfus Affair and the Millerand Case' (1899), available online at www.marxists.org, accessed 23 December 2018.

43 Ibid.

44 Rosa Luxemburg, *The Socialist Crisis in France*, available online at www.marxists.org, accessed 2 January 2019.

45 Rosa Luxemburg, *An Anti-clerical Policy of Socialism* (1903), available online at www.marxists.org, accessed 7 January 2019.

46 There has been tremendous new research into this aspect of Rosa's biography, undergone by opening old archives never before seen, by

Rory Castle Jones. See especially 'Actually, Rosa Luxemburg Was Not a Self-hating Jew', *Tablet Magazine*, www.tabletmag.com, 26 August 2016.

47 Mathilde Jacob, *Rosa Luxemburg: An Intimate Portrait* (London, 2000) p. 119.

48 Laschitza, *Rosa Luxemburg*, p. 70.

49 Ronald Florence, *Marx's Daughters: Eleanor Marx, Rosa Luxemburg, Angelica Balabanoff* (London, 1975), p. 80.

50 Frolich, *Ideas in Action*, p. 56.

51 Luxemburg, Letter to Jogiches (1898), in *The Letters of Rosa Luxemburg*, p. 46.

52 For more context of the history of the SPD see Stefan Berger, *Germany: Inventing the Nation*, (London, 2004).

53 Luxemburg, Letter to Leo Jogiches (July 1898), *The Letters of Rosa Luxemburg*, p. 82.

54 Letter to Leo Jogiches (June 1898), ibid., p. 79.

55 Luxemburg, Letter to Leo Jogiches, in *The Letters of Rosa Luxemburg*, pp. 96–7.

56 Mary-Alice Waters, Introduction to 'Social Reform or Revolution', in *Rosa Luxemburg Speaks*, ed. Mary-Alice Waters (New York, 1970), p. 33.

57 Luxemburg, 'Social Reform or Revolution', in *Rosa Luxemburg Speaks*, p. 129.

58 Ibid., p. 131.

59 Ibid., p. 132.

60 Ibid., p. 134.

61 Ibid., p. 153.

62 Ibid., p. 155.

63 Ibid., p. 156.

64 Ibid., p. 157.

65 Olga Meier, ed., *The Daughters of Karl Marx: Family Correspondence, 1866–1898* (London, 1982), p. 300.

66 This emphasis and crucial re-reading of Eleanor's place within international socialism as a whole and this particular debate is indebted to Rachel Holmes, *Eleanor Marx: A Life* (London, 2014), p. 407.

67 Rosa Luxemburg, speech to the Stuttgart Congress, 1898, available online at www.marxists.org, accessed 3 November 2018.

2 Dress Rehearsal for the Revolution

1 Quoted in G. M. Stekloff, *History of the First International*, trans. Eden and Cedar Paul (London, 1928), epigraph. For an overarching account of Marx and the First International, see Saul K. Padover, ed., *Karl Marx on the First International* (New York, 1973).

2 The historical injustice of misattributing the translation, removing credit from Eleanor Marx, was put to right in Rachel Holmes, *Eleanor Marx: A Life* (London, 2014) p. 317.

3 Quoted in Yvonne Kapp, *Eleanor Marx*, vol. II (London, 1976), p. 479.

4 Annelies Laschitza, *Rosa Luxemburg. Im Lebensrausch, trotz alledem: Eine Biographie* (Berlin, 2000, Kindle edn), p. 49.

5 G.D.H. Cole, *A History of Socialist Thought, 1889–1959* (London, 1959), p. 490.

6 Quoted in Paul Frolich, *Rosa Luxemburg: Ideas in Action* (London, 1994), p. 52.

7 Holmes, *Eleanor Marx*, p. 400.

8 The agenda of the 1893 congress stated seven themes, all of which would be crucial for Rosa Luxemburg:
   1. Steps for securing an international eight-hour working day
   2. Common action with regard to the May demonstration
   3. Political tactics of social democrats:
      Parliamentarianism and election propaganda
      Direct legislation by the people
   4. Attitude of social democracy in the event of war
   5. Protective legislation for working women
   6. National and international organization of trade unions
   7. International organization of social democrats. (IISH document)
   The entire physical archive of the papers of the Second International is held in the International Institute of Social History; it is available online at https://iisg.amsterdam/en, accessed 10 August 2018.

9 *The Letters of Rosa Luxemburg*, ed. Georg Adler, Peter Hudis and Annelies Laschitza, trans. George Shriver (London, 2013), p. 6.

10 Cole, *A History of Socialist Thought, 1889–1959* (London, 1959), p. 491.

11 Horace B. Davis, ed., *The National Question: Selected Writings by Rosa Luxemburg* (London 1976).

12 Luxemburg, Letter to Leo Jogiches (1898), in *The Letters of Rosa Luxemburg*, p. 74.

13 Luxemburg, Letter to Leo Jogiches (1900), in *The Letters of Rosa Luxemburg*, p. 128.

14 J. P. Nettl, *Rosa Luxemburg* (London, 2019), p. 842.

15 Michal Kasprzak, 'Dancing with the Devil: Rosa Luxemburg's Conception of the Nationality Question in Polish Socialism', *Critique*, XL/3 (2012), pp. 423–48, p. 426.

16 Ibid., p. 429.

17 Nettl, *Rosa Luxemburg*, p. 846.

18 Kasprzak, 'Dancing with the Devil', p. 431.

19 Ibid., p. 432.

20 Rosa Luxemburg, 'The Right of Nations to Self Determination', available at www.marxists.org, accessed 10 September 2018.

21 Luxemburg, Letter to Leo Jogiches (1905), in *The Letters of Rosa Luxemburg*, p. 207.

22 Rosa Luxemburg, 'Martinique', in *The Rosa Luxemburg Reader*, ed. Peter Hudis and Kevin B. Anderson (New York, 2004), p. 125.

23 Frolich, *Ideas in Action*, p. 141.

24 Luxemburg, Letter to Leo Jogiches (1898), in *The Letters of Rosa Luxemburg*, p. 68.

25 Luxemburg, Letter to Luise and Karl Kautsky (1899), ibid., p. 121.

26 Luxemburg, Letter to Leo Jogiches (1900), ibid., p. 124.

27 Luxemburg, Letter to Leo Jogiches, in *The Rosa Luxemburg Reader*, p. 384.

28 Ibid., p. 385.

29 Ibid.

30 Laschitza, *Rosa Luxemburg. Im Lebensrausch, trotz alledem: Eine Biographie*, p. 184.

31 The papers of the Second International, from which this account is comprised, are available online through the International Institute of Social History see https://search.iisg.amsterdam/Record/ ARCHO1299.

32 Rosa Luxemburg, 'Marxist Theory and the Proletariat', first published in *Vorwärts* (Berlin), 64 (14 March 1903), available online at www.marxists.org.

33 Rosa Luxemburg, 'Stagnation and the Progress of Marxism', in *Karl Marx: Man, Thinker and Revolutionist*, ed. D. Ryazanov (New York, 1927), p. 144.

34 Nettl, *Rosa Luxemburg*, p. 280.

35 Frolich, *Ideas in Action*, p. 91.

36 Rosa Luxemburg, 'Organizational Questions of Russian Social Democracy', in *The Rosa Luxemburg Reader*, p. 254.

37 Ibid., p. 259.

38 Ibid., p. 264.

39 Cole, *A History of Socialist Thought*, p. 493.

40 Rosa Luxemburg, 'Riot and Revolution', available online at www. marxists.org, accessed 25 January 2019.

41 Luxemburg, Letter to Luise and Karl Kautksy (1904), in *The Letters of Rosa Luxemburg*, p. 173.

42 Luxemburg, Letter to Luise Kautsky (1904), ibid., p. 175.

43 She notes taking walks without a hat – perhaps her hasty arrest did not allow her to take one into prison.

44 Luxemburg, Letter to Henriette Roland Holst (1904), in *The Letters of Rosa Luxemburg*, p. 179.

45 Luxemburg, Letter to Leo Jogiches (1898), ibid., p. 72.

46 Luxemburg, Letter to Leo Jogiches (1900), ibid., p. 130.

47 Luxemburg, Letter to Leo Jogiches (1898), ibid., p. 131.

48 Frolich, *Ideas in Action*, p. 33.

49 Eleanor Marx Aveling and Edward Aveling (1886), *The Woman Question (from a Socialist Point of View)* (London, 1886), p. 7.

50 Luxemburg, Letter to Leo Jogiches (1900), in *The Letters of Rosa Luxemburg*, p. 138.

51 Perhaps 'visits' means also any kind of communication, not only physical meetings. Luxemburg, Letter to Leo Jogiches (1905), in *The Letters of Rosa Luxemburg*, p. 199.

52 Luxemburg, Letter to Leo Jogiches (1905), ibid., p. 205.

53 Luxemburg, Letter to Leo Jogiches (1905), ibid., p. 197.

54 Luxemburg, Letter to Henriette Roland Horst (1904), ibid., p. 178.

55 Luxemburg, Letter to Henriette Roland Horst (1904), ibid., p. 179.

56 Introduction to Rosa Luxemburg, *The Complete Works of Rosa Luxemburg*, vol. III: *Political Writings 1*, ed. Peter Hudis, Axel Fair-Schulz and William A. Pelz (London, 2019), p. xvii.

57 Frolich, *Ideas in Action*, p. 121.

58 Laschitza, *Rosa Luxemburg. Im Lebensrausch, trotz alledem: Eine Biographie*, p. 234.

59 David Renton, *Classical Marxism* (London, 2002), p. 100.

60 Kasprzak, 'Dancing with the Devil', p. 444.

61 Frolich, *Ideas in Action*, p. 116.

62 Luxemburg, 'The National Question', in Davis, *The National Question: Selected Writings*, p. 92.

63 Nettl, *Rosa Luxemburg*, p. 851.

64 Ibid., p. 83.

65 Luxemburg, Letter to Mathilde Wurm (1917), in *The Letters of Rosa Luxemburg*, p. 376.

66 Rosa Luxemburg, 'Russian Women Workers in the Battle', in *The Complete Works of Rosa Luxemburg*, vol. III: *Political Writings 1: On Revolution, 1897–1905*, ed. Axel Fair-Schulz et al. (London, 2019), p. 13.

67 Rosa Luxemburg, 'Under the Sign of Social Democracy', ibid., p. 105.

68 Luxemburg, Letter to Leo Jogiches (1905), in *The Letters of Rosa Luxemburg*, p. 218.

69 Rosa Luxemburg, 'The Revolution in Russia', in *Complete Works*, vol. III, p. 63.

70 Rosa Luxemburg, 'New Year, New Struggles', ibid., p. 510.

71 Frolich, *Ideas in Action*, p. 113.

72 Nettl, *Rosa Luxemburg*, p. 316.

73 Ibid., p. 330.

74 Rosa Luxemburg, 'The Problem of the "Hundred Peoples"', ibid., p. 67.

75 Rosa Luxemburg, 'In the Bonfire Glow of the Revolution', ibid. p. 121.

3 The Last Two Men of German Social Democracy

1 J. P. Nettl, *Rosa Luxemburg* (London, 2019), p. 346.

2 Ibid., p. 369.

3 Mary-Alice Waters, Introduction, in Rosa Luxemburg, 'Mass Strike, Party and Trade Unions', in *Rosa Luxemburg Speaks*, ed. Mary-Alice Waters (New York, 1970), p. 154.

4 Paul Frolich, *Rosa Luxemburg: Ideas in Action* (London, 1994), p. 150.

5 Luxemburg, 'Mass Strike, Party and Trade Unions', p. 182.

6 Ibid., p. 184.

7 Ibid., p. 202.

8 See Lenin, 'Lecture on the 1905 Revolution', available online at www.marxists.org, accessed 4 September 2018.

9 Quoted in H. Schruer, 'The Russian Revolution of 1905 and the Origins of German Communism', *Slavonic and East European Review*, XXXIX/93 (June 1961), p. 459.

10 Rosa Luxemburg, Letter to Kostja Zetkin (1907), in *The Letters of Rosa Luxemburg*, ed. Georg Adler, Peter Hudis and Annelies Laschitza, trans. George Shriver (London, 2013), p. 246.

11 Peter Hudis, Introduction, in *The Complete Works of Rosa Luxemburg*, vol. I: *Economic Writings 1*, ed. Peter Hudis, trans. David Fernbach, Joseph Fracchia and George Shriver (London, 2014), p. xiii.

12 Rosa Luxemburg, 'The Party School', available online at www.marxists. org, accessed 3 March 2019.

13 Hudis, Introduction, in *Complete Works*, vol. I, p. xii.

14 Rosi Wolfstein quoted in Jörn Schütrumpf, *Rosa Luxemburg; or, The Price of Freedom* (Berlin, 2008), p. 44.

15 Ibid.

16 Hudis, Introduction, in *Complete Works*, vol. I, p. xiii.

17 Rosa's epistolary practice was ongoing even though often her interlocutors would have been in the same city or active in the same circles; her commitment to letter writing did not arise always out of geographical necessity. See ibid., p. xix.

18 Ibid., p. vi.

19 Rosa Luxemburg, 'What is Political Economy?', in *Complete Works*, vol. I, p. 86.

20 Ibid., p. 90.

21 Ibid., p. 141.

22 Ibid.

23 Ibid., p. 95.

24 Ibid., p. 99.

25 Ibid., p. 100.

26 Ibid., p. 195.

27 Mathilde Jacob, *Rosa Luxemburg: An Intimate Portrait* (London, 2000), p. 70.

28 Ibid., p. 25.

29 Luxemburg, Letter to Kostja Zetkin (1907), in *The Letters of Rosa Luxemburg*, p. 241.

30 Schütrumpf, *The Price of Freedom*, p. 15.

31 Luxemburg, Letter to Kostja Zetkin (1908), ibid., p. 262.

32 Luxemburg, Letter to Kostja Zetkin (1911), ibid., p. 306.

33 Luxemburg, Letter to Kostja Zetkin (1908), ibid., p. 258.

34 Luxemburg, Letter to Kostja Zetkin (1909), ibid., p. 286.

35 Luxemburg, Letter to Kostja Zetkin (1907), ibid., p. 239.

36 Joseph Stalin, 'The London Congress of the Russian Social-Democratic Labour Party, June 20 and July 10', available online at www.marxists. org, accessed 7 April 2019.

37 Luxemburg, Letter to Kostja Zetkin (1911), in *The Letters of Rosa Luxemburg*, p. 298.

38 Luxemburg, Letter to Luise Kautsky (1917), ibid., p. 365.

39 Schütrumpf, *The Price of Freedom*, p. 21.

40 Raya Dunayevskaya, *Rosa Luxemburg, Women's Liberation and Marx's Philosophy of Revolution* (Atlantic Highlands, NJ, 1984), p. 27.

41 South German and Trade Union leaders quoted in Nettl, *Rosa Luxemburg*, p. 153.

42 Ankica Čakardić, 'Luxemburg's Critique of Bourgeois Feminism and Early Social Reproduction Theory', in *Historical Materialism*, available online at www.historicalmaterialism.org, accessed 6 May 2019.

43 Rosa Levine-Meyer, *Levine: The Life of a Revolutionary* (Farnborough, 1973), p. 69.

44 Luxemburg, Letter to Emile Vandervelde (1910), in *The Letters of Rosa Luxemburg*, p. 295.

45 Rosa Luxemburg, 'Women's Suffrage and Class Struggle', in *The Rosa Luxemburg Reader*, ed. Peter Hudis and Kevin Anderson (New York, 2004), p. 238.

46 Ibid.

47 Ibid., p. 239.

48 Ibid., p. 240.

49 Ibid., p. 242.

50 Karl Marx, Preface to *Capital: Critique of Political Economy* (London, 1990).

51 David Harvey, *A Companion to Marx's Capital* (London, 2010), pp. 89–90.

52 Ben Fine and Alfredo Saad-Filho, *Introduction to Capital* (London, 2016), p. 22.

53 Ibid., p. 23.

54 Ibid.

55 Karl Marx and Friedrich Engels, *Correspondence* (London, 1934), letter 99.

56 Cited in Frolich, *Ideas in Action*, p. 148.

57 As long as surplus value is contained in the form of the commodity, however, it is useless to the capitalist. It must be transformed into money.

58 Rosa Luxemburg, 'The Accumulation of Capital', in *The Complete Works of Rosa Luxemburg*, vol. II: *Economic Writings 2*, ed. Peter Hudis and Paul Le Blanc, trans. Nicholas Gray and George Shriver (London, 2016), p. 10.

59 Rosa Luxemburg, 'Anti-critique', in *Complete Works*, vol. II, p. 374.

60 Harvey, *A Companion to Marx's Capital*, pp. 93–4.

61 Luxemburg, *The Accumulation of Capital*, p. 325; she also quotes this passage in her 'Anti-critique', p. 445.

62 Luxemburg, 'The Accumulation of Capital', p. 342.

63 Luxemburg, 'Anti-critique', p. 448.

64 Luxemburg, 'The Accumulation of Capital', p. 298.

65 Ibid., p. 302.

66 Daniel Gaido and Manuel Quiroga, 'The Early Reception of Rosa Luxemburg's Theory of Imperialism', *Capital and Class* (2013), p. 441.

67 Ibid., p. 443.

68 Lenin embarked on his own theory of the relationship between imperialism and socialism, most notably elucidated in *Imperialism, the Highest Stage of Capitalism* (1917).

69 Quoted in Paul Le Blanc's Introduction to *Complete Works*, vol. I, p. xviii.

70 Rosa Luxemburg, 'The Mass Strike', available online at www.marxists. org, accessed 10 April 2018.

4 The Countess of Wronke Fortress

1 Rosa Luxemburg, Letter to Kostja Zetkin (1908), in *The Letters of Rosa Luxemburg*, ed. Georg Adler, Peter Hudis and Annelies Laschitza, trans. George Shriver (London, 2013), p. 252.

2 J. P. Nettl, *Rosa Luxemburg* (London, 1966), p. 376.

3 Paul Frolich, *Rosa Luxemburg: Ideas in Action* (London, 1994), p. 179.

4 Ibid., p. 80.

5 Nettl, *Rosa Luxemburg*, p. 457.

6 Rosa Luxemburg, 'The Idea of May Day on the March' [1913], available online at www.marxists.org.

7 For further context of the first Morocco crisis, see Frank C. Zagare, 'The Moroccan Crisis of 1905–1906: An Analytic Narrative', *Peace Economics, Peace Science, and Public Policy*, xxi/3 (2015), pp. 327–50.

8 Nettl, *Rosa Luxemburg*, p. 445.

9 Rosa Luxemburg, 'Concerning Morocco', in *Rosa Luxemburg: Selected Political Writings*, ed. Robert Looker (London, 1972), p. 164.

10 Ibid., p. 167.

11 Rosa Luxemburg, 'Peace Utopias', in *Rosa Luxemburg Speaks*, ed. Mary-Alice Waters (New York, 1970), p. 255.

12 Rosa Luxemburg, 'Peace Utopias' [1911], available online at www.marxists.org.

13 Luxemburg, 'Peace Utopias', in *Rosa Luxemburg Speaks*, p. 256.

14 Ibid.

15 Annelies Laschitza, *Rosa Luxemburg. Im Lebensrausch, trotz alledem: Eine Biographie* (Berlin, 2000, Kindle edn), p. 396.

16 Ibid., p. 34.

17 Mathilde Jacob, *Rosa Luxemburg: An Intimate Portrait* (London, 2000), p. 26.

18 William A. Peltz, *Spartakusbund and the German Working Class Movement, 1914–1919* (New York, 1988), p. 29.

19 Jacob, *An Intimate Portrait*, p. 122.

20 Ibid., p. 23.

21 Peltz, *Spartakusbund*, p. 21.

22 Ibid., p. 72.

23 Jacob, *An Intimate Portrait*, p. 44.

24 Grunwald Henning, *The Rosa Luxemburg Trials of 1914 and the Emergence of the Ideal Type of the Weimar Party Lawyer* (Oxford, 2012), p. 2.

25 Ibid., p. 3.

26 Quoted in Nettl, *Rosa Luxemburg*, p. 83; Nettl has submitted the entire speech as an appendix to his biography.

27 Paul Levi, *In the Footsteps of Rosa Luxemburg: Selected Writings*, ed. David Fernbach (Chicago, IL, 2012), pp. 2–3.

28 Quoted ibid., p. 4.

29 Luxemburg, Letter to Paul Levi (1914), in *The Letters of Rosa Luxemburg*, p. 330.

30 Quoted in Levi, *In the Footsteps of Rosa Luxemburg*, p. 4.

31 Jacob, *An Intimate Portrait*, p. 51.

32 Luxemburg, Letter to Clara Zetkin (1916), in *The Letters of Rosa Luxemburg*, p. 356.

33 Ibid., p. 359.

34 Jacob, *An Intimate Portrait*, p. 51.

35 Ibid., p. 60.

36 Luxemburg, 'What Is Political Economy?', footnote on Rahel Varnhagen and Marwitz, p. 80.

37 Frolich, *Ideas in Action*, p. 24.

38 Luxemburg, Letter to Leo Jogiches (1898), in *The Letters of Rosa Luxemburg*, p. 82.

39 Jörn Schütrumpf, *Rosa Luxemburg; or, The Price of Freedom* (Berlin, 2008), p. 34.

40 Raya Dunayevskaya, *Rosa Luxemburg, Women's Liberation and Marx's Philosophy of Revolution* (Atlantic Highlands, NJ, 1984), epigraph. In some translations the word 'Mensch' is used instead of human.

41 Luxemburg, Letter to Hans Diefenbach (1917), in *The Letters of Rosa Luxemburg*, p. 438.

42 Luxemburg, Letter to Sophie Liebknecht (1917), available online at www.marxists.org.

43 Luxemburg, Letter to Sophie Liebknecht (August 1917), in *The Letters of Rosa Luxemburg* p. 432.

44 Luxemburg, Letter to Sophie Liebknecht (May 1917), ibid., p. 412.

45 Luxemburg, Letter to Rosi Wolfstein (March 1918), ibid., p. 459.

46 Luxemburg, Letter to Luise Kautksy (January 1917), ibid., p. 369.

47 It seems because of her unique status at the time of the arrest that she was given that option.

48 Luxemburg, Letter to Sophie Liebknecht (1917), in *The Letters of Rosa Luxemburg*, p. 414.

49 Luxemburg, Letter to Sophie Liebknecht (May 1917), available online at www.marxists.org.

50 Luxemburg, Letter to Sophie Liebknecht (December 1917), in *The Letters of Rosa Luxemburg*, p. 457.

51 Her affectionate nickname for Sophie Liebknecht. Rosa invented intimate names for many of her most consistent interlocutors.

52 Luxemburg, Letter to Sophie Liebknecht (1917), in *The Letters of Rosa Luxemburg*, p. 431.

53 Luxemburg, Letter to Martha Rosenbaum (February 1917), ibid., p. 370.

54 Rosa Luxemburg, 'Stagnation and the Progress of Marxism', in *Rosa Luxemburg Speaks*, p. 110.

55 Quoted in Subhoranjan Dasgupta, 'Rosa Luxemburg's Response to and Critique of Creativity and Culture', available online at www2.chuo-u.ac.jp.

56 Rosa Luxemburg, 'The Spirit of Russian Literature: Life of Korolenko', in *Rosa Luxemburg Speaks*, p. 341.

57 Ibid., p. 342.

58 Ibid., p. 344.

59 Ibid., p. 356.

60 Ibid., p. 346.

61 Ibid., p. 348.

62 Ibid., p. 349.

63 Ibid., p. 359.

64 Rosa Luxemburg, 'Against Capital Punishment', in *Rosa Luxemburg Speaks*, p. 398.

65 Ibid., p. 398.

66 Ibid.

67 Rosa Luxemburg, 'Life of Korolenko', p. 354.

68 Ibid., p. 354.

69 This is short for Niunia, a nickname she gave herself when writing to Kostja Zetkin.

70 Luxemburg, Letter to Kostja Zetkin (1912), in *The Letters of Rosa Luxemburg*, p. 319.

71 Jacob, *An Intimate Portrait*, p. 71.

72 Luxemburg, 'Life of Korolenko', p. 354.

73 Luxemburg, Letter to Clara Zetkin (1917), in *The Letters of Rosa Luxemburg*, p. 445.

74 Luxemburg, Letter to Sophie Liebknecht (1917), ibid., p. 451.

75 Ibid.

76 Luxemburg, Letter to Hans Diefenbach (1914), ibid., p. 337.

77 Luxemburg, Letter to Camille Husymans (1914), ibid., p. 342.

78 Rosa Luxemburg, 'Rebuilding the International', in *Luxemburg: Selected Political Writings*, p. 197.

79 Ibid., p. 204.

80 Michal Kasprzak, 'Dancing with the Devil: Rosa Luxemburg's Conception of the Nationality Question in Polish Socialism', *Critique*, XL/3 (2012), p. 437.

81   Nettl, *Rosa Luxemburg*, p. 853.

82   Ibid., p. 849.

83   Far earlier, in a letter from 1905, Rosa writes on the inability to speak
     more than one language as a barrier for internationalism, and the fact
     that all nations should unite to support the Russian Revolution, letter
     to Henriette Roland Holst (1905), in *The Letters of Rosa Luxemburg*,
     p. 187.

84   Rosa Luxemburg, 'Junius Pamphlet', in *The Rosa Luxemburg Reader*,
     ed. Peter Hudis and Kevin B. Anderson (New York, 2004), p. 313.

85   Ibid., p. 314.

86   Ibid., p. 316.

87   Ibid., p. 320.

88   This is in fact a misattribution, and this quote is derived from Chapter
     Four of Kautksy's *Erfurt Programme: A Discussion of Fundamentals*,
     where he writes: 'if indeed the socialist commonwealth were an
     impossibility, then mankind would be cut off from all further
     economic development. In that event modern society would decay,
     as did the Roman empire nearly two thousand years ago, and finally
     relapse into barbarism . . . as things stand today capitalist civilization
     cannot continue; we must either move forward into socialism or fall
     back into barbarism.' Karl Kautsky, *The Class Struggle* (London, 2018),
     p. 104.

89   Luxemburg, 'Junius Pamphlet', p. 321.

90   Ibid., p. 325.

91   Ibid., p. 328.

92   Ibid., p. 341.

93   Ibid.

5   Ultimate Revolutionary Duty

 1   Quoted in John Rees, 'In Defense of October', *International Socialism*,
     LII (Autumn 1991), p. 9.

 2   For further accounts of the Russian Revolution debunking conservative
     myths around it see, for instance, Neil Faulkner, *A People's History of the
     Russian Revolution* (London, 2017).

 3   Lenin, *The April Theses* (Moscow, 1985).

4 Rosa Luxemburg, Letter to Hans Diefenbach (March 1917), in *The Letters of Rosa Luxemburg*, ed. Georg Adler, Peter Hudis and Annelies Laschitza, trans. George Shriver (London, 2013), p. 381.

5 Luxemburg, Letter to Marta Rosenbaum (November 1917) in *The Letters of Rosa Luxemburg*, p. 441.

6 Ibid.

7 Luxemburg, Letter to Martha Rosenbaum (February 1917), ibid., p. 370.

8 J. P. Nettl, *Rosa Luxemburg* (London, 2019), p. 21.

9 Rosa Luxemburg, 'The Old Mole', in *Rosa Luxemburg: Selected Political Writings*, ed. Robert Looker (London, 1972), p. 227.

10 Ibid., p. 234.

11 Luxemburg, Letter to Mathilde Wurm (1917), in *The Letters of Rosa Luxemburg*, p. 374.

12 Luxemburg, 'The Russian Revolution', in *Rosa Luxemburg Speaks*, ed. Mary-Alice Waters (New York, 1970), p. 367.

13 Ibid., p. 367.

14 Luxemburg, Letter to Frank Mehring (1917), in *The Letters of Rosa Luxemburg*, p. 439.

15 Luxemburg, 'The Russian Revolution'.

16 Ibid.

17 Ibid., p. 389.

18 Ibid., p. 390.

19 Nettl, *Rosa Luxemburg*, p. 858.

20 Ibid.

21 It must be noted that another fierce, outlawing woman critiqued Lenin and yet endorsed the Russian Revolution and spread its message in England, and that was Sylvia Pankhurst. See Rachel Holmes, *Sylvia Pankhurst: Natural Born Rebel* (London, 2020); Katherine Connelly, *Sylvia Pankhurst: Suffragette, Socialist and Scourge of Empire* (London, 2013).

22 This is expounded by Luxemburg specialist Ottokar Luban in Rosa Luxemburg's 'Critique of Lenin's Ultra Centralistic Party Concept and of the Bolshevik Revolution', *Critique*, XL/3 (2012), pp. 357–65, especially pp. 363–5.

23 Luxemburg, 'The Russian Revolution', p. 391.

24 Charles F. Elliott, 'Lenin, Rosa Luxemburg and the Dilemma of the Non-Revolutionary Proletariat', *Midwest Journal of Political Science*, IX/4 (November 1965), p. 338.

25 Another conceptual issue which both Lenin and Luxemburg handle here from different perspectives, and is also raised by her attitude to self-determination, is the place of the state in the Marxist tradition. Lenin iterated in a one-sided way an argument from Marx that a new state form was necessary to secure political domination of the proletariat. Bob Jessop, 'Statism', *Historical Materialism*, xv/1 (2007), p. 240.

26 Jan Valtin, *Out of the Night: The Memoir of Richard Julius Herman Krebs Alias Jan Valtin* (Oakland, ca, 2004), p. 7.

27 For an excellent account of 'bottom-up history', see William A. Peltz, *A People's History of the German Revolution* (London, 2018), and *The Spartakusbund and the German Working Class, 1914–1919* (Lewiston, me, 1988), p. 126.

28 Mathilde Jacob, *Rosa Luxemburg: An Intimate Portrait* (London, 2000), p. 92.

29 Luxemburg, Letter to Clara Zetkin (1918), in *The Letters of Rosa Luxemburg*, p. 487.

30 See Eric D. Weisz, *Creating German Communism, 1890–1990: From Popular Protests to Socialist State* (Princeton, nj, 1997), p. 91.

31 Luxemburg, Letter to Clara Zetkin (November 1918), in *The Letters of Rosa Luxemburg*, p. 480.

32 Ibid.

33 Luxemburg, 'Oh! How German is this Revolution', available online at www.marxists.org.

34 Ibid.

35 Rosa Luxemburg, 'The Acheron in Motion', in *Luxemburg: Selected Political Writings*, p. 274.

36 Luxemburg, 'The Transformation of Society', in *The Rosa Luxemburg Reader*, ed. Peter Hudis and Kevin Anderson (New York, 2004), p. 346.

37 Rosa Luxemburg, 'What Does the Spartacus League Want?', ibid., p. 349.

38 Rosa Luxemburg, 'Our Program and Political Situation', ibid., p. 368.

39 Peltz, ,*The Spartakusbund and the German Working Class, 1914–1919*, p. 147.

40 Nettl, *Rosa Luxemburg*, p. 711.

41 Quoted in Peltz, *The Spartakusbund*, p. 47.

42 Luxemburg, Letter to Lenin (1918), in *The Letters of Rosa Luxemburg*, p. 486.

43 Luxemburg, Letter to Clara Zetkin (26 December 1918), ibid., p. 489.

44 Luxemburg, Letter to Clara Zetkin (December 1918), ibid., p. 489.

45 Peltz, *The Spartakusbund*, p. 70.

46 Luxemburg, 'Our Program and Political Situation', p. 372.

47 Quoted in Rob Sewell, *Germany, 1918–1933: Socialism or Barbarism* (London, 2018).

48 Jacob, *An Intimate Portrait*, p. 98.

49 Nettl, *Rosa Luxemburg*, p. 763.

50 Luxemburg, Letter to Clara Zetkin (1919), in *The Letters of Rosa Luxemburg*, p. 493.

51 Luxemburg, 'Order Reigns in Berlin', in *The Rosa Luxemburg Reader*, p. 377.

52 Luxemburg, 'Order Reigns in Berlin', p. 378.

53 Ibid.

54 The events of 15 January 1919 have been recounted many times, and often in contradictory accounts. I draw here on the most extensive work written by Klaus Gietinger and recently translated into English, *The Murder of Rosa Luxemburg* (London, 2019). I shall turn to the debates and historical inaccuracies in some tellings of these events in the following chapter, as the struggles and confrontations that led to Rosa's untimely death haunted her afterlife.

55 Luxemburg, Letter to Hans Diefenbach (1917), in *The Letters of Rosa Luxemburg*, p. 405.

56 Gietinger, *The Murder of Rosa Luxemburg*, p. 39.

57 Ibid., p. 38.

58 Goethe, *Faust*, ed. and trans. David Luke (Oxford, 2008), p. 146.

59 Luxemburg, Letter to Leo Jogiches (1898), in *The Letters of Rosa Luxemburg*, p. 80.

60 Luxemburg, Letter to Luise Kautsky (1917), ibid., p. 392.

61 Nettl, *Rosa Luxemburg*, p. 779.

62 Luxemburg, Letter to Clara Zetkin (1919) in *The Letters of Rosa Luxemburg*, p. 492.

6 Discord Marching On

1 Mathilde Jacob, *Rosa Luxemburg: An Intimate Portrait* (London, 2000), p. 123.

2 Rosa Luxemburg, 'The Spirit of Literature: The Life of Korolenko', in *Rosa Luxemburg Speaks*, ed. Mary-Alice Waters (New York, 1970)p. 358

3 Clara Zetkin, 'On the Anniversary of the Death of Two Socialist Martyrs', *Workers' Dreadnought*, 15 January 1921, available online at the British Newspaper Archive, www.britishnewspaperarchive.co.uk, accessed 10 December 2019.

4 For further context of this argument see Nigel Jones, *A Brief History of the Birth of the Nazis: How the Freikorps Blazed a Trail for Hitler* (London, 2004).

5 Clara Zetkin, 'Fascism Must Be Defeated', in *Collected Writings*, ed. Philip S. Foner (Chicago, IL, 2014), p. 172.

6 Ibid., p. 174.

7 Paul Frolich, *Rosa Luxemburg: Ideas in Action* (London, 1994), p. 307.

8 Letter to Clara Zetkin in Jacob, *An Intimate Portrait*, p. 130.

9 Luise Kautsky, Letters to Rosa Luxemburg, available online at www.marxists.org.

10 Jacob, *An Intimate Portrait*, p. 25.

11 Eric D. Weiz, '"Rosa Luxemburg Belongs to Us!" German Communism and the Luxemburg Legacy', *Central European History*, XXVII/1 (1994), p. 32.

12 Ibid., p. 45.

13 Eric Blanc, 'The Rosa Luxemburg Myth: A Critique of Luxemburg's Politics in Poland (1893–1919)', *Historical Materialism*, XXV/4 (2017), pp. 3–36.

14 Stefan Berger, *Germany: Inventing the Nation*, (London, 2004), p. 218.

15 Jörn Schütrumpf, *Rosa Luxemburg; or, The Price of Freedom* (Berlin, 2008), p. 9.

16 Ibid., p. 10.

17 Tony Cliff, 'Rosa Luxemburg's Place in History', available online at www.marxists.org, accessed 20 January 2019.

18 Georg Lukacs, 'The Marxism of Rosa Luxemburg', available online at www.marxists.org, accessed 24 January 2019.

19 Michael Brie, 'Critical Reception of the *Accumulation of Capital*', in *Rosa Luxemburg: A Permanent Challenge for Political Economy*, ed. Judith

Dellheim and Frieder Otto Wolf (London, 2016), pp. 261–303, available online at www.researchgate.net, p. 261.

20 Kanishka Chowdhury, 'Rosa Luxemburg's *The Accumulation of Capital*, Postcolonial Theory, and the Problem of Present Day Imperialisms', *New Formations*, 94 (2018), p. 151.

21 Peter Hudis, 'Non-linear Pathways to Social Transformation: Rosa Luxemburg and the Post-colonial Condition', *New Formations*, 94 (2018), p. 63.

22 Ibid., p. 73.

23 Ibid., p. 79.

24 Helen Scott, 'Capitalism in "all Corners of the Earth": Luxemburg and Globalization', *New Formations*, 94 (2018).

25 Ankica Čakardić, 'From Theory of Accumulation to Social-reproduction Theory: A Case for Luxemburgian Feminism', *Historical Materialism*, xxv/4 (2017), p. 442.

26 Ibid., p. 443.

27 Ibid., p. 444.

28 Raya Dunayevskaya, *Rosa Luxemburg, Women's Liberation and Marx's Philosophy of Revolution* (Atlantic Highlands, NJ, 1984), p. 60.

29 She specifically critiques Nettl here for referring to those years in Luxemburg's life as 'the lost years'.

30 Dunayevskaya, *Women's Liberation and Marx's Philosophy of Revolution*, p. 85.

31 Barbara Hahn, *The Jewess Pallas Athena: This too a Theory of Modernity* (Princeton, NJ, 2016), p. 110.

32 Ibid., p. 114.

33 Hannah Arendt, 'Rosa Luxemburg', in *Men in Dark Times* (New York, 1975), p. 38.

34 Ibid., p. 46.

35 Elisabeth Young-Breuhl, *Hannah Arendt: For Love of the World* (New Haven, CT, 2004), p. 361.

36 Simone Frieling, *Rebellinnen: Hannah Arendt, Rosa Luxemburg und Simone Weil* (Berlin, 2018).

37 Quoted in Barbara Harlow, 'Looked Class, Talked Red: Towards a Bio-bibliography of Ruth First', *Race and Class*, LX/3 (2019), p. 45.

38 Dov Khenin and Dani Filc, *What Is To Be Done Now?* (Tel Aviv, 2019).

39 Paul Le Blanc, 'Rosa Luxemburg and the Heart of Darkness', *New Formations*, 94 (2018), p. 138.

40 Ibid., p. 137.
41 Ibid., p. 140.
42 Luxemburg, Letter to Robert and Mathilde Seidel (1898), in *The Letters of Rosa Luxemburg*, p. 58.
43 Luxemburg, Letter to Kostja Zetkin (1915), ibid., p. 350.

Select Bibliography

The Complete Works of Rosa Luxemburg, published by Verso Books, will make available, for the first time in any language, everything she wrote – books, essays, articles, speeches, letters and manuscripts – in seventeen volumes, newly translated from German, Polish and Russian originals. Three volumes, in addition to the six-hundred-page companion volume *The Letters of Rosa Luxemburg*, have been published so far.

Volumes that have already appeared in the series:

The Letters of Rosa Luxemburg, ed. Georg Adler, Peter Hudis and Annelies Laschitza, trans. George Shriver (London, 2013)
The Complete Works of Rosa Luxemburg, vol. I: *Economic Writings 1*, ed. Peter Hudis, trans. David Fernbach, Joseph Fracchia and George Shriver (London, 2014)
The Complete Works of Rosa Luxemburg, vol. II: *Economic Writings 2*, ed. Peter Hudis and Paul Le Blanc, trans. Nicholas Gray and George Shriver (London, 2016)
The Complete Works of Rosa Luxemburg, vol. III: *Political Writings 1: On Revolution, 1897–1905*, ed. Axel Fair-Schulz et al. (London, 2019)

Many works by Rosa Luxemburg are available online free of charge on Marxists Internet Archive, a peer-reviewed source:
https://marxists.org/archive/luxemburg/index.htm

Readers and select writings by Luxemburg in English

Davis, Horace B., ed, *The National Question: Selected Writings by Rosa Luxemburg* (London, 1976)

Hudis, Peter, and Kevin Anderson, eds, *The Rosa Luxemburg Reader*
    (New York, 2004)
Le Blanc, Paul, and Helen C. Scott, eds, *Socialism or Barbarism: The Selected*
    Writings of Rosa Luxemburg (London, 2010)
Looker, Robert, ed., *Rosa Luxemburg: Selected Political Writings*
    (London, 1972)
Waters, Mary-Alice, *Rosa Luxemburg Speaks* (New York, 1970)

Works about Rosa Luxemburg

Čakardić, Ankica, 'Like a Clap of Thunder, Three Essays on Rosa
    Luxemburg', published by the Rosa Luxemburg Stiftung, available
    online at www.rosalux.de
Dunayevskaya, Raya, *Rosa Luxemburg, Women's Liberation and Marx's*
    Philosophy of Revolution (Atlantic Highlands, NJ, 1984),
Ettinger, Elzbieta, *Comrade and Lover: Letters to Leo Jogiches* (Cambridge, MA,
    1979)
—, *Rosa Luxemburg: A Life* (London, 1987)
Evans, Kate, *Red Rosa* (London, 2015)
Frieling, Simone, *Rebellinnen: Hannah Arendt, Rosa Luxemburg und Simone*
    Weil (Berlin, 2018)
Frolich, Paul, *Rosa Luxemburg: Ideas in Action* (London, 1994)
Geras, Norman, *The Legacy of Rosa Luxemburg* (London, 1983)
Gietinger, Klaus, *The Murder of Rosa Luxemburg* (London, 2019)
Hahn, Barbara, *The Jewess Pallas Athena: This Too a Theory of Modernity*
    (Princeton, NJ, 2016)
Jacob, Mathilde, *Rosa Luxemburg: An Intimate Portrait* (London, 2000)
Laschitza, Annelies, *Rosa Luxemburg. Im Lebensrausch, trotz alledem: Eine*
    Biographie, (Berlin, 2000, Kindle edn)
Le Blanc, Paul, *Living Flame: The Revolutionary Passion of Rosa Luxemburg*
    (Chicago, IL, 2020)
Levi, Paul, *In the Footsteps of Rosa Luxemburg: Selected Writings*, ed. David
    Fernbach (Chicago, IL, 2012)
Nettl, J. P., *Rosa Luxemburg* (London, 2019)
Rose, Jaqueline, *Women in Dark Times* (London, 2014)
Schutumpf, Jorn, *Rosa Luxemburg; or, The Price of Freedom* (Berlin, 2004)

Works by and about Rosa Luxemburg's context and contemporaries

Bernstein, Eduard, *Eduard Bernstein on Social Democracy and International Politics*, ed. Marius Ostrowski (Cham, 2018)

Cole, G.D.H., *A History of Socialist Thought, 1889–1959* (London, 1959)

Holmes, Rachel, *Eleanor Marx: A Life* (London, 2014)

Lenin, *Collected Works*, vol. I–III (London, 2017–18)

Levine-Meyer, Rosa, *Levine: The Life of a Revolutionary* (Farnborough, 1973)

Muldoon, James, *Council Democracy: Towards a Democratic Socialist Politics* (London, 2018)

—, *The German Revolution and Political Theory*, ed. Gaard Kets and James Muldoon (Cham, 2019)

Peltz, William A., *A People's History of the German Revolution, 1918–1919* (London, 1919)

—, *Spartakusbund and the German Working Class Movement, 1914–1919* (Studies in German Thought and History) (Lewiston, NY, 1988)

Renton, David, *Classical Marxism* (London, 2002)

Service, Robert, *Lenin: A Biography* (Boston, MA, 2000)

Sewell, Rob, *Germany, 1918–1933: Socialism or Barbarism* (London, 2018)

Valtin, Jan, *Out of the Night: The Memoir of Richard Julius Herman Krebs Alias Jan Valtin* (Chico, CA, 2004)

Weisz, Eric D., *Creating German Communism, 1890–1990: From Popular Protests to Socialist State* (Princeton, NJ, 1997)

Zetkin, Clara, *Selected Writings*, ed. Philip S. Foner, with an introduction by Angela Davis and foreword by Rosalyn Baxandall, 2nd edn (Chicago, IL, 2015)

Acknowledgements

Thank you to everyone at Reaktion Books for their work on this book. Biggest thanks go towards my editor Vivian Constantinopoulos. Her vision guided me in writing this book and her work on the various stages has not only supported the process of writing but inspired it greatly. Thank you to the vibrant and generous Rosa Luxemburg community: Paul Le Blanc for inspiration and support; Rory Castle-Jones who illuminated Rosa's early life and its continuity for me greatly; Ankica Čakardić especially for being Rosa's comrade-sister and demystifying the woman question for me; Henry Holland, for rigour and enthusiasm. Rida Vaquas for wonderful conversations. A very special thank you goes to Luxemburg scholar Helen Scott; as well as Peter Hudis, the general editor of the *Complete Works of Rosa Luxemburg*, who helped me tremendously in the process of writing and supplied ample knowledge and critical insights. Their own work on Rosa was deeply significant for the book. Kate Evans, whose work was transformative for my understanding of Luxemburg, for her unwavering solidarity and inspiration on how to understand a Clap of Thunder. Jodi Dean, a consummate comrade, for talking with me on the Lenin-Luxemburg debate, for inspiring me greatly in your example in radical thought and action. I am immensely grateful to everyone at the International Institute of Social History in Amsterdam, and in particular the archival team who shared expertise and aided in the process of researching this book from its inception. A special thank you to Pepijn Brandon, Luxemburg expert and Senior Fellow at the Institute, for his generous guidance and encouragement.

The Rosa Luxemburg Stiftung carries Rosa's work into the twenty-first century and provides a sphere for discussions of her work in our contemporary times. I am grateful for support received in various ways from different branches of the Stiftung, and especially would like to thank Albert Scharenberg, the Director of the Historical Centre for Democratic Socialism at Rosa Luxemburg Stiftung, Berlin, who warmly supported me through the early days of writing and for including me in the centenary commemoration of Rosa's death, which made the process of writing very special. Thank you: Maresi Starzmann in the New York office, who curated an exceptional exhibition of Rosa's herbarium and for her conversation and support. A special thank you goes also to Tsafrir Cohen, director of RLS in Tel Aviv.

Thank you for reasons you all know: Tara Bergin, Katherine Connelly, Lucy Grig and Rosa Hayes, Leah Cox, Sneha Krishnan. Emmy Toulson (mine and Rosa's number one comrade). Blakeley White-McGuire, Rosa's Chosen One, for ethical example and for teaching me how to listen to birdsong better. Hannah Arendt noted the significance of Rosa's peer group for her life, and I would be lost without my select 'tribe' in Israel: Yoni Bar-Or, Lee Peled, Adi Shoham, Tamara Sharon-Ross and Hodaya Slutzky-Kashtan.

This book was written in heightened political times and I would like to acknowledge the inspiration of my activist family who work ceaselessly in stopping our current descent into barbarism: David Hamblin, Sarah James, Hannah Plant and Jan Wadrup. Rosa spent her life arguing against trade union leaders and yet I would like to thank two personally; I was lucky to see a truly inspirational campaign of socialism from below take on, and I'd like to acknowledge Jo Grady, president elect of UCU, for proving that trade union leaders can be radical and sincere. Barbara Plant, President of GMB, has been an inspiration in solidarity and acting with our sisters in the past for improving the life of sisters in the present.

Rosa Luxemburg had to create her own space for thinking, writing and acting in the world. Thank you to leaders of our time who keep carving that space for others to follow. Lisa Appignanesi, whose work on memory and history has transformed my understanding of possibilities within the written word, for inspiration and generosity beyond measure. Shami Chakrabarti for her uncompromising ethical exemplar in life-long commitment to social justice. Her work is transformative for those of us continuing Rosa Luxemburg's commitment to humanism and progressive politics. Rachel Holmes, whose own writing radically changed the way I perceived understanding social justice and writing; an unwavering role model in being a sister-comrade to revolutionary women past and present. Helena Kennedy, my exemplar in all that is good and just in the world, a role model in standing up for what is right while epitomizing humanity.

I thank my entire family for their support and encouragement. My father, Harold Mills, did not live to see the publication of this book, but his humanity, generosity and principle are inscribed in every line I have ever written and will ever write. I was fortunate to be raised with the example of my aunt, Tirza Posner, and my mother, Gabriella Mills, who embody humanism for me and taught me to seek that which is right and not to turn a blind eye to injustice. My grandmother, Annemarie (Miriam) Posner, a fiercely independent and truly original personality, is missed by us all every day. I dedicate this book to them, the Jewish women who made me who I am today.

All mistakes in the book, however, are my own.

Photo Acknowledgements

The author and publishers wish to express their thanks to the below sources of illustrative material and/or permission to reproduce it.

Courtesy Kate Evans and Verso Books: p. 177; International Institute of Social History (Amsterdam): pp. 17, 35, 53, 54, 56, 60, 70, 75, 80, 83, 85, 86, 94, 100 (Rosa Luxemburg Papers), 107, 113, 115, 117, 118 (Rosa Luxemburg Papers), 122 (Rosa Luxemburg Papers), 147, 149, 162; Dana Mills: pp. 178, 179.